RUDOLF STEINER (1861–1925) called his spiritual philosophy 'anthroposophy', meaning 'wisdom of the human being'. As a highly developed seer, he based his work on direct knowledge and perception of spiritual dimensions. He initiated a modern and universal 'science of spirit', accessible to anyone willing to exercise clear and unprejudiced thinking. From his spiritual investigations Steiner provided suggestions for the renewal of many activities, including education (both general and special), agriculture, medicine, economics, architecture, science, philosophy, religion and the arts. Today there are thousands of schools, clinics, farms and other organizations involved in practical work based on his principles. His many published works feature his research into the spiritual nature of the human being, the evolution of the world and humanity, and methods of personal development. Steiner wrote some 30 books and delivered over 6000 lectures across Europe. In 1924 he founded the General Anthroposophical Society, which today has branches throughout the world.

SIX STEPS IN SELF-DEVELOPMENT

The 'Supplementary Exercises'

RUDOLF STEINER

Selected and compiled by Ateş Baydur

RUDOLF STEINER PRESS

Translated by Matthew Barton

Rudolf Steiner Press
Hillside House, The Square
Forest Row, RH18 5ES

www.rudolfsteinerpress.com

Published by Rudolf Steiner Press 2010

Originally published in German under the title *Die Nebenübungen, Sechs Schritte zur Selbsterziehung* by Rudolf Steiner Verlag, Dornach, in 2007. This authorized translation is published by permission of the Rudolf Steiner Nachlassverwaltung, Dornach

A catalogue record for this book is available from the British Library

ISBN: 978 1 85584 237 3

Cover by Andrew Morgan Design
Typeset by DP Photosetting, Neath, West Glamorgan
Printed and bound in Malta by Gutenberg Press

Mixed Sources
Product group from well-managed forests, and other controlled sources
www.fsc.org Cert no. TT-CoC-002424
© 1996 Forest Stewardship Council
FSC

The paper used for this book is FSC-certified and totally chlorine-free. FSC (the Forest Stewardship Council) is an international network to promote responsible management of the world's forests.

Contents

Note to the Reader

Given that this volume is largely made up of quotations from Rudolf Steiner's works, in order to keep a consistent flow to the language, tone and terminology we judged it best to translate afresh Rudolf Steiner's words from the latest and most accurate German editions. To aid English readers in finding English editions of the relevant works, a list of published translations is given on page 87.

('GA' stands for *Gesamtausgabe* or Collected Works of Rudolf Steiner in the original German.)

About this book

The so-called supplementary exercises are of key importance in the path of knowledge and self-development which Rudolf Steiner proposed. He gave them to pupils right from the start of his work as an esoteric teacher, suggesting that they should be carried out *alongside* the primary meditation and concentration exercises. He repeatedly highlighted their significance, saying that they were capable of balancing any harmful effects of meditative practice and of lending inner certainty and security to the soul. Those for whom these supplementary exercises have become a constant companion know that they are also, in their own right, of inestimable value in their beneficial and wholesome effect on daily life.

In six stages these exercises enable one to practise qualities we can summarize as: control of thoughts, initiative of will, equanimity, positivity, open-mindedness and equilibrium of soul. The path involved is one of self-knowledge and self-development, thus opening a source of inner strength and psychological health that soon make themselves felt in daily life. As such, continual practice can become a natural, self-evident need.

Ever new discoveries await those who engage in these supplementary exercises: less an experience of developing new qualities that are merely added to our existing person-ality but more, it seems, as if each separate exercise places us into a spiritual reality in which we now participate. An aspect of the self that was previously concealed is activated and becomes a real point of departure for the way we lead our life. Such practice can then be experienced as a process of spiritual birth.

The supplementary exercises form an organism. Each of them presupposes capacities acquired in the previous stages. Thus progress relies on having properly understood and practised what went before. The present compilation of as near as possible all Rudolf Steiner's relevant comments on these exercises can be helpful here. Diverse aspects of repeated yet often somewhat differently formulated comments can offer ever new stimulus for the specific way in which we approach and carry out these exercises.

I have attempted to give comprehensive quotations wherever Steiner offers detailed guidance for carrying out the supplementary exercises; and I have made a representative selection from his numerous other comments about their importance.

This compilation offers excerpts without their full, original context. As long as one remembers this, the new juxtapositions presented here can be very helpful for illuminating each exercise.

After *Occult Science* was published in 1910, Rudolf Steiner mostly referred people to that book for guidance on the supplementary exercises. For this reason, extracts from it are placed at the beginning of each chapter. This is followed in a first section by passages drawn from the rest of Steiner's written oeuvre. In a second section, in chronological order, come passages on the supplementary exercises taken from lectures. A third section cites comments made during esoteric classes. This latter section starts in each case with excerpts from the written instructions he recorded in 1906, entitled '*General requirements that each person who wishes to undergo esoteric development must make of himself*' (abbreviated here as 'general requirements' directly after the relevant passage).

At various places in Steiner's complete works, he merely lists the supplementary exercises—but such enumeration can also be informative since he often gives the exercises slightly different names. I have therefore given a selection of such references at the beginning of each chapter.

The final chapter contains passages chosen to illumine specific aspects of the supplementary exercises.

The nature of the lecture transcripts can be seen by referring to the complete edition of Rudolf Steiner's works. In particular one should note that the esoteric classes given within the Esoteric School between 1904 and 1914 were retrospectively recorded recollections by participants. Different recollections of the same classes show the extent to which these deviate from each other.

Ateş Baydur

Prelude

An appropriate path of schooling will refer to certain qualities to be acquired by those who wish, through practice, to seek their way into higher worlds. Such qualities are, above all: the soul's mastery of its thoughts, of its will and its feelings. The manner in which this mastery can be practically achieved has two aims: firstly our psyche should be informed by certainty, security and equilibrium to such a degree that we continue to retain these qualities even when a second I is born from us. Then, also, this second I should receive strength and inner stability for its further path.

(GA 13, 1910)[1]

Below I will characterize the conditions that must underpin esoteric development. No one should think that he can make progress by any outward or inward means without fulfilling these conditions. All meditation and concentration exercises, and suchlike, are worthless and may even be harmful in a certain sense if we do not regulate our lives in accordance with these conditions. We can't receive powers: we can only unfold those that already lie within us. Due to outer and inner hindrances, they do not develop by themselves. The outer hindrances are removed by following the rules given below, while the inner hindrances are addressed through specific instructions relating to meditation and concentration, etc.

(General requirements, October 1906)[2]

First supplementary exercise

Control of thoughts
Regulating the course of thinking
Mastery of thought processes
Objectivity
Concentration
Focused thought

Objectivity is of primary importance for human thinking when engaged in the path of spiritual schooling. In the physical and sensory world, life is the great teacher of objectivity for the human I. If the soul were to let thoughts wander hither and thither at random, it would soon have to accept correction from life's realities or else find itself at odds with them. The soul must think in accordance with these realities. But when we direct our attention away from the physical and sensory world, the latter's inevitable corrections fall away. If our thinking is then unable to act as its own corrector, it will inevitably lose itself in arbitrary flights of fancy. For this reason the spiritual pupil must practise thinking that determines its own direction and goal. Inner stability and the capacity to stay focused on a particular subject[3] is needed for educating our thinking. Corresponding 'thinking exercises' should not therefore be focused on distant and complex subjects but on simple ones that are near to hand. If we overcome our resistance and, over several months, turn our thoughts for at least five minutes each day to a mundane object (such as a pin or pencil, etc.), excluding all other, unrelated thoughts as we do so, we have already achieved a good deal. (You can take a new object each day, or keep to the same one for several days.) Even someone whose academic training means that he regards himself as a 'thinker' should not consider it beneath him to prepare his spiritual schooling in this way. If we focus our thoughts for a while on something very familiar to us, we can be sure that we start thinking in an appropriately objective way. Someone who asks himself what a pencil is made of, how its materials are produced or prepared, how they are then assembled, or how and when a pencil was first invented—and so on and so forth—is surely adapting his ideas to reality much more than someone who thinks about the origins of man or the meaning of life.

Simple thinking exercises, far more than complex, scholarly ideas, make it easier for us to properly conceive such things as Saturn, Sun and Moon evolution.[4] Initially it is not a question of thinking *about* this or that subject, but of thinking objectively and appropriately, and invoking inner strength. If we develop the capacity for objective thinking in relation to an easily grasped, sensory, physical process, then thinking will acquire the tendency to be objective when it is no longer subject to the sway of the physical, sensory world and its laws. At the same time we rid ourselves of the habit of letting our thoughts wander erratically.

(GA 13, 1910)[5]

The first thing of this kind that the esoteric pupil undertakes is to regulate his thought processes (so-called 'control of thoughts'). Just as the sixteen-petalled lotus[6] unfolds through

true, meaningful thoughts, so the twelve-petalled lotus develops by inner mastery of one's thinking processes. Thoughts that flit about randomly and are combined in a purely accidental way rather than purposefully or logically, spoil the form of this lotus flower. The more one thought proceeds from another, and the more anything illogical is avoided, the better this sense organ acquires its appropriate form. When the esoteric pupil hears illogical thoughts expressed, he immediately corrects them inwardly. But he ought not to withdraw unlovingly from what may be illogical surroundings in order to cultivate his own development. Nor should he desire to immediately remedy everything illogical in his environment. Instead, very quietly and inwardly, he will bring the thoughts storming at him from without into a logical train of thought. And he will take pains to continually follow such trains of thought in his own thinking.
(GA 10, 1905)[7]

One achieves control of the world of thoughts if one takes pains to counter what is, in most people, an arbitrary flitting, a surging and subsiding, of thoughts and feelings. In daily life we tend not to be in charge of our thoughts but are driven by them. This is quite natural, for life drives us, and as active participants in it we have to give ourselves over to life's activity. This will inevitably be so in ordinary life. But if we wish to rise to a higher world, we must make space for at least short periods when we take mastery of our world of thoughts and feelings. We can do so by placing a thought into the clear focus of our soul in complete inner freedom, in contrast to the usual process whereby thoughts and images impinge on us from without. We can try to keep all arbitrarily surfacing thoughts and feelings at a distance, only connecting with our original thought what we wish to connect with it. Such an exercise has a beneficial effect on the soul, and thus also on the body. It endows the latter with such harmony that it can fend off harmful influences even when the soul does not directly act upon it.

(GA 12, 1906)[8]

a) Control of thoughts. The *chela*[9] cannot allow himself to view things from only one angle. We grasp an idea, consider it to be true—yet it is only true in one aspect or from one perspective. Later we must also view it from the opposite perspective, and see the other side of every coin. Only by this means do we learn to check one thought against another.

(Summer 1903)[10]

Then we have to develop a range of qualities. First and foremost this involves gaining mastery of our thoughts, our thought processes and sequences. This is called 'control of thoughts'. Just reflect for a moment how thoughts flit and flutter about in us, like will-o'-the-wisps: here an impression, there another, and each new impression alters our thoughts. It is not true to say that we guide and direct our thoughts. Rather they control us completely. We must however set aside a certain period of the day when we focus on a particular thought and allow no other thought to intrude and hold sway over us. Then, for a while, we ourselves hold the reins of our life of thinking.

(7 December 1905)[11]

Today people are given up to every passing thought. However, we ourselves must control the reins of thinking, and then we will introduce rhythm into ourselves.
(19 April 1906)[12]

Firstly: to focus one's thinking power on a single object, and allow it to dwell there. This is called acquiring control of one's thoughts.
(30 May 1906)[13]

Firstly: control of thoughts; in other words, the pupil should only entertain those thoughts which he himself wishes to have. These exercises require much patience and persistence. But if we practise for only five minutes a day, this is already significant for our inner life.
(9 July 1906)[14]

Control of thoughts. This involves—at least during short periods in the day—not allowing anything and everything to flit through the soul but instead letting calmness inform our train of thought. One thinks of a certain concept, placing this into the focus of one's thinking, and then intentionally attaching to this concept all other thoughts in a corresponding logical sequence. Even if we do this for only a minute, it is already of great importance for the rhythm of the physical and etheric body.
(2 September 1906)[15]

Firstly: Dispensing with the habit of flighty thinking. This sounds easy but is in fact difficult. Outer impressions drive and propel us. For at least five minutes each day we should gain complete mastery over our train of thought. As an exercise one can for example try to place a single idea at the centre of one's attention. Then, whatever other arbitrary thoughts suggest themselves, I try not to connect with this idea anything except what I freely and intentionally choose to connect with it. Such exercises should take the most diverse subjects as their starting point. After some time, a more controlled kind of thinking will develop, and this will come to expression in greater precision in speech.

(19 September 1906)[16]

Firstly we should acquire the capacity to strictly control our thinking. We must practise placing a thought at the centre of our soul life—the more intensely the better. We must stay with the chosen subject, and attach all further thoughts sequentially to it. This exercise must be done for at least five minutes each day. The more one does it the better, though one should not overtax oneself.

(22 February 1907)[17]

Concentration is something one must practise from the very beginning, concentration of thought life. Just reflect for a moment how thoughts flit about in you from morning till evening! From here, there and everywhere, thoughts come to you and pull you after them. Now, as a Rosicrucian pupil[18] you must set aside periods of the day when you master your thoughts, when you take a subject for reflection that is as uninteresting as possible. This will be of enormous benefit.

The time it takes is of no importance; what you need for this is energy, patience and persistence.
(29 June 1907)[19]

To sit down, take an ordinary thought and allow no other thought to intrude, and to think this thought as intensively as possible, dismissing all other thoughts, requires a certain inner effort. This effort is the important thing. The subject of reflection itself should not interest and absorb us. For instance, it would be easy to think about Napoleon, but very difficult to think, say, uninterruptedly about a match for a longish period. That is the important thing. Then you will find that after a while this gives you a certain inner strength and stability. Whether this exercise has achieved what it should will become apparent as inner experience.
(7 November 1907)[20]

Concentration of thoughts means strongly harnessing thoughts, integrating and combining one's thoughts in a concentrated fashion [...]
(29 March 1913)[21]

★

The first condition is to acquire completely clear thinking. To do this, we have to free ourselves from the usual flitting about of thoughts, even if only for a brief moment during the day, say five minutes (the longer, the better). We have to master our world of thoughts. We cannot do so if outward circumstances, profession, traditions of any kind, social relationships and even our particular nationality or the time of day, etc. determine the thoughts we have and how we spin them out. During moments of quiet reflection we must intentionally free our souls from our usual, daily trains of thought, and by our own initiative place a thought at the centre of our attention. Don't imagine that this has to be an outstanding or especially interesting thought; the esoteric effect will actually be better achieved by starting with a thought that is as uninteresting and unimportant as possible. This better stimulates the independent activity of thinking, whereas a thought of intrinsic interest itself urges our thinking forwards. It is better to practise control of thoughts by focusing on a pin than on Napoleon. Do it like this: start from the chosen thought and, through nothing but your own inner initiative, sequentially add all that can objectively be connected with it. At the end of this period of reflection, the thought should still retain as much colour and life in your soul as at the outset. Do this exercise day after day for at least a month. You can start with a new thought each day or continue with the same one for several days. At the end of such an exercise, try to become fully aware of the inner sense of stability and security that you will soon notice if you pay subtle attention to it; and then end the exercise by thinking of your head and the middle of your back (brain and spinal cord) as if you would pour this sense of stability into those parts of the body.

(General requirements, October 1906)[22]

The first of these supplementary exercises is *control of thoughts.* Take a subject that you try to think about for five minutes without any other thought intervening. Then a

certain feeling should arise, which you pour into your body. The less interesting the subject of reflection is, the more useful it will be for this purpose, since holding it in your attention for five minutes will require greater effort.
(20 January 1907)[23]

The first supplementary exercise involves finding an undisturbed period at some point in the day during which you place a thought at the centre of your thinking and stay with it for at least five minutes. To start with it is best to choose as simple and apparently insignificant a thought as possible, then calmly, sequentially relate to it whatever can be thought about it or in connection with it. If you choose an interesting subject, your thoughts will associate with it for a long time quite by themselves. But if you choose a match, say, you will have to make strenuous efforts to keep thinking about it. And it is precisely this effort which wakens the soul's powers. You can think as follows. What does a match look like? What different types of match exist? How are they manufactured? What are they used for? Where are they kept? What harm can they do? And so on and so forth. By doing this exercise, after a while you will notice a sense of inner security and stability. This is a quite specific feeling. Try to become fully aware of it and then, as if it were water, pour it into your head and spine. You must do this exercise daily for at least four weeks. You can also do it for months until you feel that it bears good fruit.
(29 January 1907)[24]

1. *Control of thoughts:* You should set aside at least five minutes a day to reflect on a subject that is as insignificant as

possible, one that does not intrinsically interest you, logically connecting with it everything that can be thought about it. It is important for the subject to have little significance for you, since forcing yourself to stay with it for a long time is precisely what awakens the soul's slumbering capacities. After a while you will notice in yourself a sense of stability and security. Do not imagine, however, that this sense will overwhelm you. No, it is a very delicate, subtle feeling that one must hearken and attend to. A person who says he definitely cannot feel this sense within him can be compared to someone who sets out to look for a very small, delicate object among many other objects. He searches, but only superficially, and overlooks the thing he is looking for. You have to hearken very quietly and attentively, then you will sense this feeling, chiefly in the front part of the head. Once you locate it, imagine pouring it into your brain and spine. Gradually you will have the impression of rays streaming back from your forehead and descending into the spine.

(6 June 1907)[25]

1. *Control of thoughts:* Take an insignificant subject for reflection—since what matters is the effort that draws up inner powers and not our interest. Examples given are: a match, a hairpin, a fountain pen, etc. We can ask: how did the object first come about, what is it made of, how is it manufactured, where is it made, what would happen if it did not exist in the world?

The more you exert yourself and have to overcome your own resistance, the better it is.

It is the same as when the eye first developed!

Spend five minutes fixing your attention on an object that does not interest you—that is the important thing; then you will be relieved when you can let it go again.
(6 June 1907)[26]

1. *Concentration.* Take a subject for reflection, preferably an insignificant one that holds no intrinsic interest for you but which you have to fix your attention upon. Think about it for at least five minutes without moving on to think of other things, always keeping focused on the same train of thought. You can prepare yourself by finding out more about the subject in advance. After a few days you can choose a different subject.

This exercise awakens in the pupil a sense of stability by activating the chakra between the eyebrows. One should direct this feeling from there through the brain into the spine.
(13 August 1908)[27]

Why is it that we know our physical body so little? It is because we live in it and only perceive it feelingly. Because we use our eyes to see with, we cannot observe them. The esotericist must arrive at the point of withdrawing with his soul and spirit and freeing himself from the physical. Then he will become able to observe his physical body. We can support ourselves in this by concentrating our thoughts as far as possible in one focused point, and then submerging ourselves in this point, living within it for a while. This kind of concentration strengthens the power of thinking, and thereby we can gradually manage to observe our physical body.
(2 January 1914)[28]

1. Through concentrated thinking, through our concentration exercises, we gradually become aware of our physical body as of something external to us: we feel it as something that stands there and in a certain sense belongs to us.
(2 January 1914)[29]

In the first supplementary exercise, involving concentration, we occupy ourselves entirely with only one subject of reflection that we have chosen—the more mundane the better. We connect one thought after another with this and then, when the exercise is over, it is good not to throw ourselves immediately into busy activity but to allow at least a quarter of an hour to pass. If we do this, then—not immediately, not after a week or a month but after some time of continued and serious practice—we will feel as though something wavelike enters the head, the brain: as though the etheric body is coming back into the brain in successive waves.
(7 February 1914)[30]

Second supplementary exercise

Control of will
Control of actions
Mastery of will impulses
The soul's mastery of its will
Initiative in actions
Power of initiative

Such a person should also achieve mastery of the will in the
same way that he masters the world of thoughts. Again, it is
life in the physical, sensory world that dominates here,
invoking this or that need in the human being which the will
feels moved to satisfy. In higher schooling we must accustom
ourselves to obeying our own orders rigorously. If we do so,
we will be less and less open to desiring insignificant things.
The unsatisfying lack of stability in our will life, however,
derives from a desire for things we have no clear conception
of realizing. This dissatisfaction can bring disorder into our
whole life of heart and mind at the point when a higher I is
about to emerge from the soul. A good exercise is to com-
mand oneself to carry out a particular action at a particular
time of day, for several months on end. Gradually one will
become able to precisely dictate the time and manner in
which one carries this out. In this way we can raise ourselves
above the ill effects of 'wanting this and desiring that' without
having any conception of realizing it.

A great individual (Goethe) puts into the mouth of a female

visionary the words: 'Him I love who desires the impossible' (*Faust*, Part II). And Goethe likewise says: 'Living in the idea means treating the impossible as though it were possible' (*Proverbs in Prose*). This should not however be taken as an objection to what is intended here. The prompting which Goethe and his visionary (Manto) pursue can only be fulfilled by someone who has first schooled himself by desiring what is possible; and who then, through his strengthened will, becomes able to engage with what is 'impossible' in such a way that his will transforms it into something possible.
(GA 13, 1910)[31]

A second thing is to introduce the same kind of consequentiality into our actions (control of actions). All volatility and disharmony in our actions spoil the lotus flower I spoke of. After doing something, the esoteric pupil orders his subsequent action accordingly, so that it proceeds logically from the initial action. Someone who acts from different motives or in a different way today than he did yesterday will never develop the kind of purposeful action I have described.
(GA 10, 1905)[32]

Control of actions consists in similarly regulating these actions in inner freedom. A good way to start is to do something regularly which ordinary life does not require us to do. Normally life impels us to take certain actions. Yet the smallest action we accomplish out of our own intrinsic initiative has a greater effect of the kind described than everything which life externally drives us to do.
(GA 12, 1906)[33]

★

b) Control of actions. We live and act in the material realm, and within temporal sequences. We can only grasp a small part of the wealth of phenomena in the world, and our actions bind us to a certain limited and transient sphere. Daily meditation helps the *chela* to configure and control his actions. He will look only for what is lasting in them and place value only on the deeds through which he can help his fellow human beings and serve their higher development. He will raise the wealth of phenomena back to the highest unity.
(Summer 1903)[34]

The second thing necessary is to relate to our own actions in a similar way, or in other words practise control of our actions. We need at least to accomplish actions which no outer cause requires of us. Every action which our profession, job or position in life requires of us does not lead us deeper into higher life. Higher life depends on intimate, subtle things—such as deciding to do an initial thing which springs from our own most inherent initiative, even if this is an entirely insignificant action. All other types of action contribute nothing to higher development.
(7 December 1905)[35]

Accomplishing actions from one's own initiative; undertaking every action out of one's own intrinsic motive: this brings the kind of composure the soul needs.
(19 April 1906)[36]

Secondly: acting likewise in relation to all activities whether great or small: mastering and regulating them, bringing them under the will's control. All of them must subsequently proceed from inner initiative. This is the meaning of control of one's actions.
(30 May 1906)[37]

Secondly: initiative in one's actions. These should be something that originate in and emerge from one's own soul.
(9 July 1906)[38]

Initiative in action means we should compel ourselves to actions, however insignificant, which arise from our own initiative, tasks we impose on ourselves. Most causes of action lie in family circumstances, education, profession and so forth. Just consider how little actually proceeds from our own initiative! Now we should spend a short time allowing actions to proceed from our own initiative. These don't have to be important things at all: entirely unimportant actions fulfil the same purpose.
(2 September 1906)[39]

Secondly: initiative in action. Many lack this capacity entirely, for normally they are pushed into some profession at an early age and this accounts for the greater part of their actions. Most of our actions are externally determined. Someone who seeks initiation, therefore, should make it a matter of keen importance to regularly accomplish an action at a particular time of day which arises from his own inner motives, even if such action is basically insignificant.
(19 September 1906)[40]

Secondly, initiative in action is needed. This involves the pupil accomplishing an action daily that arises from his own most intrinsic initiative. It is sufficient for this to be a quite small, unimportant action, such as watering flowers. After a while one then undertakes a different action.
(22 February 1907)[41]

Then one should move on to taking the initiative for actions that one otherwise would certainly not have performed. It might well be an entirely insignificant action. The significance of the action is not the important thing, but the fact that it is entirely one's own, based on one's own inmost initiative. A gentleman I suggested this to told me some time later that he had taken seven steps forwards and seven steps backwards in his office each day, at the same time picturing to himself evolution and involution. Excellent! The scope of the action is not important but the fact that it is motivated by one's inmost initiative.

I also told some friends about this exercise, suggesting as an example that they might water flowers if this was not a habitual action for them. And what happened? When I visited these friends, I found them all watering flowers! This was the most wrong-headed thing they could do: it wasn't *my* suggestion they were supposed to realize, but one they decided on themselves alone. If you do this for a long period of time you will discover its inner effect. Such things harmonize and balance everything in the physical and etheric body in such a way that these two inherently resonate, and no longer need much improvement—so that the astral body can withdraw a part of its forces.
(7 November 1907)[42]

Developing and consolidating a certain initiative of the will
[...]
(29 March 1913)[43]

★

After practising for about a month in this way, add another
task. Try to think of some action that one would otherwise
certainly never undertake in the normal course of life. Now
make this a self-imposed duty to be carried out each day. It
will therefore be good if you choose an action that can be
performed for as long as possible each day. Once again it is
better to start with an unimportant action, one that you more
or less have to force yourself to take—for instance, to water a
flower at a certain time every day. After a while, a second
such action should be added to the first, then later a third and
so on: as many as you can manage without neglecting all your
other daily tasks. This exercise should again last a month.
But during this second month you should as far as possible
continue with the first exercise as well, though no longer as
the exclusive duty it was during the first month. Yet you
should not overlook it, for otherwise you would soon notice
the fruits of the first month fading, and the old roller-coaster
of uncontrolled thoughts starting again. In general you need
to take care that the fruits once gained are never lost again.
Having accomplished this second exercise for self-initiated
action, you will become subtly aware of a sense in the soul of
inner motivation; and you should pour this feeling as it were
into your body, so that it streams down from the head and
over the heart.
(General requirements, October 1906)[44]

The second exercise is called initiative in actions. This must involve an action one has to compel oneself to take.
(20 January 1907)[45]

Secondly, we should practise initiative in actions. To do this we choose actions we would not otherwise perform, and which we undertake only for the sake of this exercise. Exercises that are as simple as possible, which we have to force ourselves to do, are the most effective to begin with. Again one soon notices a particular feeling, a sense of stability and an urge to be active. We should lead this feeling to full awareness, then pour it like water from the head down to the heart so as to completely incorporate it. This exercise should be done at a particular time of day, and should continue for at least four weeks.
(29 January 1907)[46]

2. Initiative in actions: Choose an action that you decide on for yourself. For instance, it will be useless to simply 'follow instructions' by watering a flower—the example I gave— since the action must be one born from your own initiative. Thus you need to think of it for yourself. In doing this exercise a feeling will soon become apparent—roughly 'I can accomplish something', 'I can accomplish more than I used to be able to', 'I sense the urge to act'. Really you will feel this in the whole upper part of your body. Then try to let this feeling flow towards the heart.
(6 June 1907)[47]

2. Initiative in actions: a few of my pupils did this exercise wrongly by simply performing the example I suggested, of

watering flowers, instead of—as I intended—accomplishing an action that one would not otherwise perform in life. It has to be an action drawn from one's own soul. Each person has to find the appropriate initiative for himself. The usefulness of the action is not important, but instead the fact that it is not demanded by external circumstances or accomplished out of goodness of heart. Thus, giving money to a poor person will not do, as this is an ethically motivated action. It must instead arise from one's own, intrinsic initiative and against one's own resistance: this is activity that forms our occult organs.

(6 June 1907)[48]

2. Exercising the will. Undertake each day to do something at a particular time, again an inherently insignificant action. This exercise likewise gives you stability.

(13 August 1908)[49]

We must also come to know our etheric body. This is still harder since the etheric body is not enclosed in our skin like the physical body but is, rather, a fine weft that sends its currents everywhere out into the external world and likewise receives impressions from all that occurs in the external world, often in a way that we are quite unconscious of.

We can learn to sense the etheric body by proper practice of the second supplementary exercise, for the will. Usually, external impressions drive us to act. We see a flower in a meadow and, since it pleases us, we may stretch out a hand to pluck it. As an esotericist, in contrast, we must come to be able to do this or that without external stimulus, solely out of an inner impulse that we give ourselves consciously. Then we can perceive that it is the etheric body which causes the hand to move. Thus we can feel our etheric body awaken.

Through this awakening etheric body we gradually learn to experience ourselves in the etheric world. In reality, every time we move—for instance if I grasp an object or knock against it—this is an attack on the outer world. The non-esotericist has no inkling of this, for he is protected from such knowledge by the Guardian of the Threshold; but the esotericist gradually makes his etheric body independent, so that it experiences itself in the etheric world. His organs become more sensitive, and he increasingly acquires a sense of the fact that every space is filled not just with physical objects but with a countless number of elemental beings who make themselves felt through pricking, prodding and burning. In this elemental etheric world one has to make space for oneself everywhere through will impulses such as stretching, withdrawing, pushing, walking forwards, etc., and such movements must occur with the full awareness that one wishes this out of one's inmost being. That is the second thing: initiative in actions. Someone who cannot make space for himself in this etheric world through his initiating will can achieve as little in this world as someone in the physical world who tries to dance on a stage crowded with chairs. First the chairs have to be removed. The second exercise teaches us how to do this in the spirit.

(2 January 1914)[50]

II. Through initiative in action (mastery of will impulses) we become aware of our etheric body. As long as we simply want or desire something through the stimuli that reach us from the external world, we do not sense the currents in the etheric body that come into movement when we act. We have to create space around ourselves if we wish to do something out of ourselves, like someone who, wishing to dance, has to move tables and chairs away first. As soon as we do something out of ourselves, not triggered by something from without, we make ourselves strong within, sending our will from within outwards and feeling the currents and movements which must accompany every action in the etheric world. Every movement is an attack on the outer world; we become increasingly aware that every space is filled with a host of elemental beings. When we act from within outwards we come up against these elemental beings and thereby become aware of our etheric body.

(2 January 1914)[51]

In the second supplementary exercise, for initiative, in which one harnesses the will for a certain activity at quite particular times, one will gradually come to feel after the exercise as if one had been active in one's etheric body. One has the sense of having feelingly found oneself in one's etheric body. A feeling of profound reverence and piety then enters the soul of the meditant.

(7 February 1914)[52]

Third supplementary exercise

Composure
Composure towards joy and suffering
Control of feeling
The soul's mastery of its feelings
Equanimity
Soul equilibrium
Acquiring equilibrium in life
Fortitude
Forbearance
Tolerance

In relation to our world of feelings, the soul embarking on spiritual schooling should develop a certain composure. For this it is necessary that the soul masters its expressions of delight and suffering, joy and pain. Certain prejudices can arise specifically in regard to the acquisition of this quality. One might imagine one would grow dull and unresponsive to one's surroundings by not 'taking pleasure in what is pleasing or feeling pain at what is painful'. But this is not what is needed. What is pleasing should give the soul pleasure, and what is sad should pain it. Yet the soul should come to hold sway over *expressions* of joy and pain, delight and aversion. If we strive to do this, we will soon notice that we do not become duller but on the contrary more receptive than previously to all that is pleasing and painful in our surroundings. This does however require attending carefully to oneself over a longer period, to acquire the quality involved here. We have to ensure that we fully experience joy and sorrow without losing ourselves in the process, thus involuntarily expressing what we feel. We should not suppress justified pain but involuntary tears; not aversion to a bad action but the blind rage of anger; not attention to a danger but useless fearfulness and so on. Only through such an exercise does the spiritual pupil develop the composure of heart and mind necessary to prevent the soul producing a kind of doppelgänger that lives a second, unhealthy life alongside the higher I when the latter is born and comes into effect. We should not allow ourselves to be deceived in relation to these things. It may appear to some that they already have a certain equilibrium in their ordinary lives, and that this exercise is not therefore necessary. Such a person has double need of it. We can actually be calm and composed in relation to the ordinary circumstances of life yet, on rising to a higher world, can find ourselves all the more devoid of equilibrium—the lack of which was merely suppressed before. We have to recognize that spiritual schooling is less about what we *appear* to possess initially than about regular and careful *practice* of what we need to develop. However contradictory this statement may seem, it is true nevertheless. While life may have developed this or that capacity in us, spiritual schooling is served by the inner qualities *we ourselves develop*. If life has taught us to be excitable, we should rid ourselves of excitability; if life has taught us equanimity, however, our self-education should shake us up so as to make our soul expressions correspond to the impressions we receive. Anyone unable to laugh at anything is as little in control of his life as someone who continually and uncontrollably finds things to laugh at.

(GA 13, 1910)[53]

The sixth thing is to acquire a certain equilibrium in life (equanimity). The esoteric pupil strives to maintain an even mood, whether affected by suffering or pleasure. He sheds the habit of swinging back and forth between 'sky-high rejoicing' and deep gloom. Misfortune or danger find him as well fore-armed as happiness and good fortune.

(GA 10, 1905)[54]

Fortitude involves keeping at a distance the mood swings we can describe as 'sky-high rejoicing' and 'deeply downcast'. We are driven back and forth between all sorts of moods. Enjoyment cheers us while pain depresses us. This is natural and justified. But if you seek the path to higher knowledge you must be able to moderate your expressions of pleasure and pain, developing what I would call 'fortitude'. You must be able to give yourself only in moderation to pleasure-inducing impressions and likewise to pain-evoking ones, always walking on through both with dignity. Nothing should overpower you or make you lose your composure. This does not breed lack of feeling but makes us a firm island amidst the waves of life that rise and fall around us. We always have ourselves in hand.

(GA 12, 1906)[55]

★

d) Forbearance. Meeting fortune or misfortune with equanimity, not allowing them to become forces that determine and influence us. Not allowing ourselves to be pushed out of kilter by joy and pain. Keeping ourselves free of all outer influences and effects, and pursuing our own thread. *(Summer 1903)*[56]

The next thing, the third we should strive for, is fortitude. People swing back and forth between joy and pain, at one moment being sky-high with joy, and the next down-in-the-dumps. They allow the waves of life, of joy and pain, to carry them to one extreme or the other; yet they should acquire equanimity, composure. The greatest suffering, the greatest joys should not unsettle them: they must stand firm, develop fortitude. *(7 December 1905)*[57]

Fortitude: standing secure and firm, allowing suffering and joy to pass over us; to develop fortitude. Not letting joy any more than pain sidetrack us. *(19 April 1906)*[58]

Thirdly: soul equilibrium. We have to allow moderation to hold sway over both pain and joy. Goethe said that the soul in love experiences 'sky-high rejoicing' at one moment, and is 'deeply downcast' the next. The esoteric pupil must endure the greatest pleasure and the greatest pain with the same equanimity of soul. *(30 May 1906)*[59]

Thirdly: inner composure. By this means we develop a much finer sense of sympathy. *(9 July 1906)*[60]

Composure. The third thing necessary is what we can call composure. Here we learn to regulate our swinging back and forth between 'sky-high rejoicing' and being 'deeply downcast'. Whoever does not wish to do this because he thinks it will deprive him of spontaneity or artistic sensitivity will be unable to embark on esoteric schooling. Composure means mastering the greatest joy and the profoundest pain. In fact we only become fully receptive to the joys and sufferings in the world when we no longer lose ourselves in pain and pleasure, no longer immerse ourselves in them egotistically. The greatest artists have achieved the most through this composure because it enabled them to open their souls to important subtle and inner qualities.
(2 September 1906)[61]

Thirdly, the pupil should get beyond 'sky-high rejoicing' and being 'deeply downcast'. In other words, we should not give ourselves up involuntarily to every pain and joy but instead should retain our equanimity even in the face of the bitterest pain and the greatest pleasures. This certainly does not need to engender dullness or lack of feeling. On the contrary, it develops in us a still more refined and sharpened sensitivity.
(19 September 1906)[62]

Thirdly, we must master pleasure and suffering. We must cease to be driven back and forth between 'sky-high rejoicing' and being 'down-in-the-dumps'. This actually makes us more sensitive and receptive; but we ourselves must be master, rather than being mastered by the feelings.
(22 February 1907)[63]

Then one has to master oneself in relation to pleasure and suffering. Normally we are enslaved by our feelings: we laugh when something especially funny presents itself, or cry when something sad occurs. The pupil must take himself in hand however: instead of being in thrall to his feelings he must himself master pleasure and suffering. Many people think this will dull their sensitivity, but the reverse is true. By this means we overcome pleasure and suffering—in other words, egotistic pleasure and egotistic pain. We have to find a way to, as it were, slip out of ourselves into other beings, to have sympathy with them. No one should refrain from this exercise through concern that he will grow dull; instead he will become more sensitive.
(7 November 1907)[64]

[...] a certain equilibrium between pleasure and suffering [...]
(29 March 1913)[65]

★

In the third month a new exercise should become the focus of your practice: developing a certain equilibrium in fluctuations between pleasure and pain, joy and suffering. Swinging between 'sky-high rejoicing' and being 'deeply downcast' should be consciously replaced by an even mood. You can take care that no joy carries you away, no pain floors you, no incident drives you to boundless anger or annoyance, no expectation fills you with fear or anxiety and no situation leaves you stunned or bewildered, etc. You should not fear that this exercise will render you neutral or poor in response to life. Instead you will soon notice that what occurred in you prior to this exercise is replaced by purified qualities of soul. Above all, by attending carefully you will eventually come to sense an inner calm in your body. As in the two other instances described above, you should pour this feeling into your body by letting it radiate from the heart to the hands, to the feet and finally the head. In this case, of course, this cannot be done after each individual exercise since really this is not a single exercise but an ongoing attentiveness to your inner life of soul. At least once a day you should invoke this sense of inner peace, and then practise allowing its current to emanate from the heart. Manage the exercises of months 1 and 2 in the same way that you handled the first exercise during the second month.

(General requirements, October 1906)[66]

Thirdly, overcoming pleasure and displeasure. This does not mean not feeling joy or suffering, but not allowing oneself to be ruled by them.

(20 January 1907)[67]

In the third month, or after the second practice period, one starts to put an end to all fluctuations and mood swings in one's soul life. All states of swinging between 'sky-high rejoicing' and profound gloom should fade. No pain should crush us, no joy send us spinning. Fear, excitement, consternation must vanish. By this means we develop a third feeling in us: a sense of calm equanimity which makes itself felt like inner warmth. We should focus this feeling in the

heart and from there let it stream into the hands, into the feet and then towards the head.
(29 January 1907)[68]

3. Being elevated over joy and suffering. For instance, imagine that you can feel tears rising. Then it is time to practise this exercise: you can vigorously compel yourself not to cry. The same can apply to laughing. When you feel you're going to laugh, try not to, but stay calm instead. This does not mean you shouldn't laugh any more; but you should have yourself in hand, rule over laughter and tears. And once you have managed this a couple of times, you will soon also sense a feeling of calm and equanimity. Let this feeling flow through your whole body by pouring it first from the heart into arms and hands, so that it radiates from them into deeds. Then let it stream to the feet and finally towards the head. This exercise requires serious self-observation which should be carried out for at least a quarter of an hour a day.
(6 June 1907)[69]

3. Overcoming pleasure and suffering: We must draw on our strong will to avoid being carried away by joy or suffering. We must be not the horse but the chariot driver (Plato). If tears rise in us for some reason, we should suppress them vigorously and tell ourselves: 'You are not to cry now.' The same applies to laughter. All this is conceived only for a certain period, roughly a month.
(6 June 1907)[70]

3. Developing equanimity; this means not swinging between 'sky-high rejoicing' and being 'down-in-the-dumps'. A joke

is not valued any less if one does not laugh at it uproariously; a pain is borne less egotistically if one does not hold fast to it so strongly.

This gives a sense of calm, which we should allow to stream out from the heart through arms and hands.
(13 August 1908)[71]

We should not only believe theoretically in karma; it is very hard to really feel it as consequence in difficult situations in life. The esoteric exercises can help us here, for instance the practice of composure. We should not only stand above pleasure and pain but also, in every fibre of our being, be wholly given up to the greater justice ('Lord, Thy will be done').
(14 October 1911)[72]

To become aware of our astral body we have to do precisely the opposite. We have to hold back the desires passing like waves through the astral body, and develop composure and equanimity towards them. We must create an absolute lull, absolute calm in us. Only then will we feel the external astral world impinge on our inner astral world. Just as we come up against the etheric world by intervening in it through our self-instigated will, so we feel the external astral world by remaining calm within ourselves, by bringing all desires and wishes to stillness.

Before the astral body can do this, it numbs or deafens itself by crying out. We know that pain arises when the physical and etheric bodies are not in proper contact with each other. The astral body experiences this as pain. When the young child experiences pain he cries out. He tries to outdo the pain by crying. The adult may call out: 'Ouch!' If we could succeed in making our pain stream entirely into the vibrations of the uttered tone, the latter's vibrations would give rise to such changes in the etheric body's formation that we would not experience pain, but instead it would sink down into the subconscious.

But the benevolent gods have given us a weaker disposition—and this is good, for otherwise there would be no suffering, nor any articulated speech. The esotericist must come to the point of bearing all pain, and everything that external factors trigger in him, with calm, composure and equanimity. Then he will not launch attacks on the external world (through his astral body) but the attacks turn towards him from without. But since he has developed complete composure, they only touch his physical and etheric body. The astral body remains untouched. It becomes as it were free, and we can observe it. In other words, by practising composure, I can come to know my astral body.
(2 January 1914)[73]

III. To become aware of our astral body, we have to do precisely the reverse. We have to hold back the desires surging through the astral body; instead of letting everything emanate from us, we must develop composure and balance. Then, calm within ourselves, we feel the external astral world impinge upon us. Just as we impinge on the etheric world by intervening in it at our own instigation (acting out of the will centre), so now we feel the astral world impinge upon us as we remain calm within ourselves, bringing all desires and wishes, all surging of pleasure and suffering to stillness. Before we have taught ourselves to do this, we numb or deafen ourselves to the desires that hold sway in us by crying out, we let them issue forth in tones. But because our astral body has been weakened by the gods, this later becomes articulated speech and song.

(2 January 1914)[74]

In the third supplementary exercise, for balance between joy and suffering, we should find our way into all that happens, integrating and accepting it. Then our etheric body will gradually expand into the breadths of the heavens. We will then no longer feel ourselves within our body and the whole world around us, but instead will feel our body spread out in the whole of our environment: will feel ourselves spread out, expanded and poured into worlds of spirit. We feel, find and know ourselves to be in the spiritual world.

In these three supplementary exercises we experience the two first sentences of our Rosicrucian verse:[75] how we are entirely embedded in the divine, spiritual forces, and have descended from them; and how we pour ourselves in the third exercise into the world of spirit, into the Christ. For Christ is now in the earth's aura, in the earth's atmosphere; we must let Him hold sway in us, as it were alongside and beside us.

(7 February 1914)[76]

Fourth supplementary exercise

Positivity
Positivity in judging the world
Open-mindedness
Lack of prejudice
Forbearance
Tolerance
Insight
Sense of affirmation
Trust in one's surroundings
Steadfastness

A further means to educate our thinking and feeling is by acquiring the quality we can call positivity. There is a fine legend about Christ Jesus:[77] that he passed a dead dog in the company of several other people and while these others turned aside from the ugly sight, spoke admiringly of the animal's beautiful teeth. We can practise maintaining this stance of soul towards the world. What is faulty, bad or ugly should not prevent us from finding the true, the good and the beautiful wherever it is present. One should not confuse this positivity with being devoid of all critical faculties, or with intentionally closing one's eyes to all that is bad, false or debased. Whoever admires 'a dead animal's beautiful teeth' will also see the decomposing corpse. But this corpse does not *prevent* him from seeing its beautiful teeth. One can't find the bad good or the error true, but we can come to the point of not allowing the bad to prevent us from seeing the good or the false from seeing the true.

(GA 13, 1910)[78]

The fourth thing is forbearance (tolerance) towards other people, creatures or circumstances. The esoteric pupil suppresses all superfluous criticism of what is imperfect, bad or evil, and instead seeks to understand what approaches him. Just as the sun does not withdraw its light from what is bad or evil, so he likewise does not withdraw his understanding participation. If the esoteric pupil encounters some kind of ill-conduct, he does not dismiss it with derogatory judgements, but instead accepts what is unavoidable in it and tries—as far as he is able—to bring it to a positive outcome. He views other opinions not just from his own perspective but also tries to put himself in someone else's shoes.

(GA 10, 1905)[79]

The 'sense of affirmation' is a particularly important quality. This can be developed by seeking out good, fine or useful characteristics in all things, rather than focusing primarily on what is reprehensible, ugly or contradictory. There is a lovely Persian legend about Christ which demonstrates the nature of this quality: a dead dog lies beside a path. Christ is among those passing by; and while the others turn their gaze away from the ugly sight, Christ speaks admiringly of the animal's beautiful teeth. We can feel like this towards things: in everything, even the most distasteful, an earnest seeker can find something worth acknowledging. And the fruitful aspect

of something is not what is faulty or lacking in it, but the attributes it possesses.
(GA 12, 1906)[80]

★

c) Tolerance. The *chela* will not let himself be ruled by feelings of attraction and repulsion. He will try to understand all human beings—both criminals and saints. And while he experiences things emotionally, he will judge them intellectually. What is correctly perceived from one perspective as evil can be judged from another as being necessary and coherent.
(Summer 1903)[81]

The fourth thing is to understand every creature or being. A Persian legend about Christ expresses most beautifully what this involves; it is not found in the Gospels but in Persian literature. Jesus was walking over the fields with his disciples, and on their way they found a rotting dog. The animal looked ghastly. Jesus stopped and looked admiringly at the creature, at the same time saying: 'How beautiful its teeth are.' Thus Jesus found something beautiful in the midst of what was hideous. If you strive to find something glorious everywhere in outer reality, you will see that everything has something that can be affirmed. Be like Christ who admired the beautiful teeth in a dead dog. This will lead you towards great tolerance and understanding for all things and beings.
(7 December 1905)[82]

Then one must acquire the greatest open-mindedness. This quality is diminished most of all when we highlight what is negative in things; this leads to disharmony and at the same time to exhaustion. Here we can take guidance from the Persian legend that tells how Christ Jesus and his disciples saw a dead dog lying on a road. The disciples asked their master not to concern himself with the dog, for it was so ugly. Yet Christ gazed upon it and said: 'What beautiful teeth it has.' He was seeking something beautiful in the midst of ugliness. All affirmation enlivens, all negation exhausts and kills. This is not only because an ethical power is involved in turning to the positive aspect of something, but also because affirmation enlivens us and renders the soul's faculties free and secure.

In an age such as ours, nervousness also predominates. Being nervous and highly critical belong together. The virtues I propose are there to release higher powers for human beings. Such virtues, which aim to infuse all lower impulses with a rhythmic quality, endow the soul with powers that enable it to turn towards higher development. This inner development happens in quiet seclusion.
(19 April 1906)[83]

Fourthly: positivity. The soul state that consists in seeking good in everything. A Persian legend relates that as Christ was once passing the foul-smelling corpse of a dog, his disciples turned away in disgust. But, after observing this ghastly sight, Christ said to them: 'What beautiful teeth the animal has.'
(30 May 1906)[84]

[. . .] Positivity, which enables us to draw the best aspect from everything [. . .]
(6 June 1906)[85]

Fourthly: to seek and find the positive aspect in all things and occurrences. Here I'd remind you of the beautiful legend of Christ and the dead dog.
(9 July 1906)[86]

Open-mindedness, lack of prejudice: this is how the fourth can be described. This quality involves seeing the good in all things, focusing on the positive in everything. The best example is given in a Persian legend relating to Christ. One day Christ Jesus saw a dead dog lying on his path. He stopped and observed the animal, whereas his companions turned away in disgust from this sight. But Christ Jesus said: 'Oh, what beautiful teeth the animal has!' He did not see what was bad or ugly but found something beautiful—the white teeth—even in this foul corpse. If we adopt this stance, then we can seek positive qualities, the good, in everything, and can find it everywhere too. This exerts a very powerful effect on the physical and etheric body.
(2 September 1906)[87]

Fourthly: a Persian legend about Christ Jesus should come to vivid life in us: Jesus was journeying with his disciples and passed a half-decomposed dog on the path, a ghastly sight. The disciples turned away in horror, but Christ Jesus looked lovingly upon the corpse and remarked: 'But just look at this dead animal's beautiful teeth.' The essence of this is to discover the beauty concealed even in the ugly, and in general always to seek the positive, whatever one can say 'yes' to. Even the life of the worst miscreant has light-filled moments which we should meet with insight and understanding.
(19 September 1906)[88]

Fourthly, positivity is needed. We can understand what this involves through a Persian legend about Christ Jesus. Christ was journeying with several of his disciples and they passed a dead dog that had already begun to decompose. The disciples turned away saying how ugly the animal was. But Christ stopped to look and said: 'Just look at the animal's beautiful teeth!' In other words you can seek and find something beautiful even in the most ugly, good in the most evil, and greatness in the least thing. These qualities have to be sought everywhere.
(22 February 1907)[89]

The other thing is what one can call 'positivity', which consists in seeking everywhere in life for something that can best be characterized by citing a Persian legend about Christ Jesus: When Jesus Christ was making his way one day with his disciples they found a dead and already decomposing dog by the edge of the road. The disciples, who were less developed than Christ, turned away in repugnance from the sight. Christ however stood still, observed the animal carefully and said 'But what beautiful teeth the animal has!'

However much ugliness there is in the world you can still find beauty in the ugly, a grain of truth in every untruth, a good in every evil. This does not mean relinquishing all critical faculties! People often take this to mean that they should no longer find anything bad at all . . . but what is really meant is that there is a grain of beauty in everything ugly, and something good in everything bad. This draws up the soul's higher forces. All this forms part of the preparation.
(29 June 1907)[90]

A fourth exercise is the one I can best characterize by relating a legend drawn from the life of Christ. Like many other such legends, it isn't in the Bible. It comes from Persian culture. When the disciples were journeying with Christ one day they saw the half-rotted corpse of a dog on their path. 'What foul carrion,' said the disciples, turning away in disgust. But alone among them Christ Jesus stopped, looked at the corpse and after a while remarked what beautiful teeth the animal had. He saw past the ugly, rotting corpse to the beauty of the teeth. This shows us how we can and must acquire the capacity to find the grain of beauty in all ugliness, the good concealed in all bad, the truth in all error. This quality of positivity has to be practised for some time, and gives inner harmony and rhythm.
(7 November 1907)[91]

[...] a certain positivity in one's attitude to the world [...]
(29 March 1913)[92]

★

During the fourth month we should take up what is called positivity, as a new exercise. This involves seeking always what is good, excellent, beautiful, etc. in all experiences, beings and things. This quality of soul is best characterized in a Persian legend about Christ Jesus. When he was walking along one day with his disciples they saw a dead dog by the wayside that was already half-decomposed. All the disciples turned away from this ugly sight; but Christ Jesus stopped, reflectively observed the animal and said: 'But what beautiful teeth the animal has!' Where the others saw only something ugly and repugnant, he sought the beautiful. Similarly, the esoteric pupil must try to find the positive aspect in everything that happens and in every creature or person. He will soon notice, if he does, that an ugly exterior conceals something beautiful, that a hidden beauty can be found even in a criminal, and that the divine soul is present somewhere under the surface of a madman. This exercise is somewhat related to what we can call the withholding of criticism. It does not mean calling black white or white black. But there is a difference between judging things in a way that issues merely from one's own personality, reacting accordingly in sympathy and antipathy, or the stance which enters lovingly into the other being or phenomenon and continually asks: 'Why is the other like this', or 'Why does he act as he does?' Such a stance inevitably leads to greater efforts to aid what is imperfect rather than simply criticize and find fault with it. The objection that many people's circumstances require them to find fault and judge is misplaced here, for such circumstances mean that they will be unable to undergo a proper occult schooling. Many circumstances do indeed prevail which prevent people undergoing proper and full occult training. We should not impatiently demand our own progress despite this, for we can only advance under certain specific conditions. Someone who takes a month to focus consciously on all that is positive in what he experiences will gradually notice that a feeling slips into him as though his skin became permeable on all sides and his soul opened wide to all hidden and subtle processes in his surroundings which he previously entirely failed to notice. This is the real point: to combat the lack of attention to such subtle things which all of us have. Once we notice that this feeling has entered the soul like a kind of happiness or blessedness, we should try to direct this feeling towards our heart and from there let it stream into our eyes; and from there out into space and around us. If you do this you will notice it gives you an intimate relationship with this surrounding space. It is as if you grow beyond yourself, learning to regard a part of your environment as belonging to yourself. A great deal of focused concentration is needed for this exercise, and above all acknowledgement of the fact that all stormy passions and raging emotions utterly destroy such a mood. The exercises from the first months continue in the way already suggested. *(General requirements, October 1906)*[93]

Fourthly: Seeking *positivity* in everything.
(20 January 1907)[94]

After the third exercise period we develop what can be called positivity. In everything, even the worst, most terrible or ugly, you should find what is good and beautiful, as the Persian legend about Christ and the dog teaches us. Eventually you will start to sense a feeling of inner bliss. Concentrate this feeling in your heart, let it ray towards the head and from there out through the eyes, as if trying to radiate it through the eyes.
(29 January 1907)[95]

4. *Positivity:* In everything bad look for the germ of good, in everything ugly the grain of beauty and in every criminal the spark of divinity. Then one feels as if one is expanding

beyond one's skin. This is a sense of growing larger similar to that which the etheric body has after death. If you sense this, let it ray out through your eyes, ears and the whole skin, but chiefly through the eyes.
(6 June 1907)[96]

4. *Positivity:* What is meant by this is expressed in the following legend. Christ Jesus was walking with his disciples when they saw by the roadside a dog in the last stages of decomposition. The disciples turned away in disgust and said: 'O, what an ugly beast.' But Christ Jesus stopped and looked at the corpse lovingly, then said: 'What wonderful teeth the animal has!'

Thus positivity involves drawing beauty and truth from everything and finding it even in what is most ugly, criminal, or untrue. Subtle self-observation belongs here.
(6 June 1907)[97]

4. *Seeing beauty and truth in all things.* One can think of the Persian legend of Christ Jesus who admired the beautiful teeth of a dead dog, whereas the disciples saw only ugliness. One can discover a grain of truth and beauty in everything.

Persisting in this exercise gives rise to a feeling of great joy.
(13 August 1908)[98]

Finally I also have to get to know my I. I cannot sense my I because I live within it. This is why we have to pour it out into the world. I learn to know my I through what we can call positivity (parable of the dog).

If we imitate Christ Jesus in this, instead of seeing ugliness

we immerse ourselves in everything in such a way that we find the good in it. By this means we get free of our ego and can observe it. It is love and will. Through the developed will we learn to perceive the substance of all things, which originate in God. Through love we learn to inwardly experience the nature of things. Thus, through will and love, we penetrate to insight free of the personal ego. As spiritual I we learn to immerse ourselves in the essence and substance of all things, which derive from the spiritual father ground as does our own I. Our I looks out at us from within all creation ('Swan'). The pupil reaches the stage of the 'Swan' when he can experience this.
(2 January 1914)[99]

IV. We become aware of our I by developing positivity in ourselves, by developing autonomous judgements which enable us to see beauty in even the ugliest thing.
(2 January 1914)[100]

Fifth supplementary exercise

Open-mindedness
Belief
Trust
Lack of prejudice
Continual openness
Spiritual openness for every new phenomenon
Freedom from judgement

Thinking in connection with the will undergoes a certain maturation if we try never to let what we have experienced rob us of unbiased receptivity to new experience. The spiritual pupil should lose all sense that something cannot be true because he has never heard of it before. For a certain period he should take every opportunity to allow all things, beings or people to tell him something new about themselves. We can learn something from every breeze, every leaf, the burbling of an infant if we are prepared to find a new or different point of view. However, it is easy to go too far in relation to such a capacity. At a certain age we should not ignore our past experiences. We ought to judge what we experience here and now in relation to our past experiences. We place that on one side of the scales. On the other the spiritual pupil must place an inclination to continually have new experiences. Above all he must retain belief that new experiences may contradict the old ones.

(GA 13, 1910)[101]

The fifth thing is lack of bias towards all that occurs in life. In this connection one can also speak of 'belief' or 'trust'. The esoteric pupil meets every other being with this trust, and fills himself with it in his actions. He never says to himself that he does not believe something because it contradicts his previous opinion. Instead he is willing at every moment to test his views and opinions against new ones, and correct them if necessary. He always remains receptive to all that approaches him, and trusts in the efficacy of what he undertakes. He banishes diffidence and scepticism from his soul. If he has an intention, he also has faith in the power of this intention. Hundreds of failures cannot deprive him of this faith. This is the 'faith that can move mountains'.
(GA 10, 1905)[102]

It is also important to develop the quality of 'open-mindedness'. Each person has his own experience and forms a certain number of opinions in accordance with it which become his guiding principles in life. However self-evident it is to draw on one's experiences, it is equally important for someone who wishes to develop spiritually towards higher knowledge to always keep an open mind towards everything unknown that approaches him. He will be as cautious as possible about saying that 'something can't be true'. Whatever his opinions tell him based on his past experience, he will be prepared at any moment to entertain a different opinion in response to something new he encounters. All self-love in relation to one's opinions must disappear.
(GA 12, 1906)[103]

e) Faith. The *chela* should have a free, open, unbiased heart for higher spiritual realms. Even where he does not immediately perceive a higher truth, he should have faith until he can acquire this through insight and understanding. If he were to act according to the principle of 'testing everything and retaining the best', he would establish his own judgement as a yardstick, thus placing himself above the higher spiritual realm and closing himself off from the latter.
(Summer 1903)[104]

The fifth quality is complete open-mindedness towards anything new we encounter. Most people judge the new that approaches them in terms of what they already know. If someone comes to tell them something they reply immediately: 'I have a different view.' But we should not immediately counter someone else's opinion with our own. Instead we should keep a weather eye open to discover where we may learn something new. And we can learn something new even from a young child. Even if someone were amongst the wisest of human beings, he would need to hold back his judgement and listen to others. We have to develop this capacity to listen, for it enables us to bring the greatest possible open-mindedness to bear on things. In occultism this is called 'belief': the power to avoid diluting impressions that something new makes on us by countering it with something we already possess.
(7 December 1905)[105]

Fifthly: open-mindedness. Spiritual openness to every new phenomenon; the capacity never to let the past determine our judgement.
(30 May 1906)[106]

[. . .] A stance free of prejudices [. . .]
(6 June 1906)[107]

Fifthly: open-mindedness and lack of bias. We should always allow ourselves the possibility of acknowledging new facts.
(9 July 1906)[108]

The next is faith. This means something different in esoteric terms from what we usually understand by it in ordinary speech. When we are pursuing esoteric development, we should never allow our past to determine our future. During esoteric development we must sometimes ignore what we have so far experienced, so as to be able to meet every new experience with a mood of belief or faith. The occultist must do this consciously. For example, if someone were to come along and say, 'The church tower is leaning over, it's bent down at a 45-degree angle,' anyone would reply that this can't be true. But the occultist must keep a tiny back door of belief open in his mind. He must even go so far as to be able to believe everything he encounters in the world, for otherwise he will close off his capacity to have new experiences. We have to leave ourselves open for new experiences; and by this means the physical and etheric bodies are endowed with a mood which can be compared with the lusty mood of a bird that is hatching an egg.
(2 September 1906)[109]

Fifthly, we should strive for complete freedom from prejudice. The past should never dictate our view of the future. We should not simply dismiss something new

because we have never encountered it before. One should meet new perceptions with an open mind if one wishes to become an initiate.
(19 September 1906)[110]

Fifthly, we must acquire complete open-mindedness towards all new impressions, the highest degree of receptivity. People tend to say: I have never seen or heard of such a thing, I don't believe it! We must radically rid ourselves of the habit of thinking something is impossible. We must leave a small space in our heart to believe, for instance, that the church spire is leaning at an angle if someone comes to tell us this. We must at least entertain the possibility that what we hear is true.
(22 February 1907)[111]

The fifth thing is to acquire some degree of open-mindedness in relation to anything new that we encounter in the world. We could also say that we should never allow our future to be influenced by what we are used to from the past. The phrase 'I don't believe that' must vanish from our soul. And if someone comes to tell you that the church spire has gone crooked overnight, you must find a tiny corner in your heart where you believe that this, or anything else, may be true. This does not mean you should dispense with all your critical faculties; but nothing should strike you as impossible. Someone capable of this can act significantly on his physical and etheric bodies, and by this means they enter into a rhythm that makes it possible to give the astral body at night what can be available to it through meditation and concentration. People will gradually come to true theosophy by gaining insight into why everything happens in a particular way. Those who understand the mechanism of sleep also know why such exercises should be practised.

(7 November 1907)[112]

★

In the fifth month you should then try to develop in yourself the sense of encountering every new experience with a completely open mind. Saying such things as 'I've never seen or heard that before, I don't believe it, it's an illusion' embodies an attitude that the esoteric pupil should entirely dispense with. He must be willing to encounter a completely new experience at any and every moment. All he has previously perceived as natural law, everything that has appeared possible to him, must not act as fetters that prevent him absorbing a new truth. It is radical to say so, but right nevertheless, that if someone were to come to an esoteric pupil and tell him that the spire of the local church has bent right over in the night, he should not close his mind completely to the possibility that this might be true; that his previous understanding of natural laws might have to be amended to encompass such an apparently unheard-of thing. If, in the fifth month, you pay attention to developing this attitude, you will notice a feeling slipping into you as though something comes alive, something stirs, in the space we spoke of in relation to the exercise of month four. This feeling is extraordinarily subtle and delicate. You must try to attentively grasp this subtle resonance in your surroundings and let it stream as it were through all five senses, especially

through eyes, ears and skin inasmuch as the latter contains the sense of warmth. At this stage of esoteric development one should pay less attention to impressions stirring in the lower senses of taste, smell and touch. At this stage it is not yet really possible to distinguish the numerous bad influences mixed up with the good ones in this domain, and therefore the pupil should leave this for a later stage.
(General requirements, October 1906)[113]

Fifthly: an open mind towards all experiences and phenomena.
(20 January 1907)[114]

During the fifth month practise never letting your past dictate the future. Become wholly free of prejudice, absorb everything with an open soul. If someone says to you that the church spire turned back to front in the night, instead of mocking him consider that a law of nature of which you are unaware may exist. Then you will soon get a sense as though something were streaming towards you from surrounding space. Suck this in, as it were, through eyes, ears and your whole skin.
(29 January 1907)[115]

5. *Open-mindedness:* Keep yourself flexible, always capable of absorbing something new. If someone tells you something you consider unlikely, always keep a tiny space of possibility in your heart that this might after all be true. You don't have to lose all critical faculties, for after all you can investigate and find out. You will then feel a sense of something

streaming towards you from without. Suck it in through eyes, ears and the whole skin.
(6 June 1907)[116]

5. *Open-mindedness.* Being open and unbiased is exemplified by not replying, 'No, I don't believe you, that's quite impossible,' if, for example, someone tells us that a church spire has suddenly bent over at a 45-degree angle. We have to develop a sense that nothing is impossible.
(6 June 1907)[117]

5. *Continual openness* for learning something new. We should never say, 'I've never heard such a thing, it can't be true!' Whatever we hear, we should keep an open mind at least to learning something new from it. We can learn something from children, animals, everything.

This gives one a sense of being also able to partly perceive things outside of the body.
(13 August 1908)[118]

At the fifth stage we develop *manas* or *Spirit Self.* Here we must refrain from being fixated on what we have previously seen, learned or heard. We have to learn to look afresh, meeting everything we encounter as though entirely emptied of the past. Manas can only be developed if we learn to regard all ideas we have acquired as less valuable than what we may acquire by opening ourselves to ideas streaming into us from the god-woven cosmos. Everything that surrounds us arose from these divine thoughts. Our thinking has not so far been able to find them, and things themselves conceal them. Now we learn to sense this divine aspect underlying everything like a concealed riddle. We learn increasingly to see, modestly, how little of these riddles we have so far grasped. And we learn that we must actually remove everything we have learned hitherto from our soul, that we must meet everything with an open mind, like a child, and that the divine riddles that surround us will only reveal themselves to this open, unprejudiced faculty of soul. The soul must become childlike if it is to enter the kingdom of heaven. Hidden wisdom—manas—will then stream towards the childlike soul, like a gift of grace from the world of spirit.

(2 January 1914)[119]

V. And through open-mindedness or trust, through passing from ourselves out into others so as to absorb them with an open mind, we learn to know and feel the Spirit Self.

(2 January 1914)[120]

Through open-mindedness, lack of bias—Spirit Self.

That is the highest level we can reach initially. Other exercises can then take us further.

(2 January 1914)[121]

Sixth supplementary exercise

Equilibrium of soul
Inner harmony
Harmonizing the five qualities
Steadfastness
Persistence
Perseverance
Spiritual emphasis
Certainty of direction
Composure

Thus we have named five soul qualities which the spiritual pupil should acquire through proper schooling: mastery of thinking processes, mastery of will impulses, composure in relation to pleasure and suffering, positivity in evaluating the world and an open mind to what presents itself in life. If we have practised acquiring these qualities in successive periods, we will still need to bring them into harmonious accord with one another. To establish such harmony we need to practise them together at the same time—two and two, three and one and so on.
(GA 13, 1910)[122]

The third thing is to develop perseverance. As long as he can regard a goal he has set himself to be right, the esoteric pupil does not allow himself to be diverted from this goal by some influence or other. Hindrances to achieving it are

for him an impetus to overcome them, but no reason to cease trying.
(GA 10, 1905)[123]

Once the soul has acquired the previously named five qualities, a sixth—inner equilibrium, harmony of spiritual forces—arises by itself. We must find within us something like a spiritual emphasis that gives us stability and security in relation to all that pulls us in one or another direction in life. We should not avoid experiencing everything sympathetically, allowing everything to work upon us. Rather than fleeing the tug and pull of circumstances we should do the opposite: give ourselves fully to life and, despite this, safely and securely preserve our inner equilibrium and harmony.
(GA 12, 1906)[124]

★

f) Balance. As the result of all the other soul capacities, the last would arise as balance, as certainty of direction, as equilibrium of soul. The *chela* sets his own direction.
(Summer 1903)[125]

The sixth quality is the one we acquire naturally once we have developed the other capacities. This is inner harmony. The person who has the other qualities also has inner harmony.
(7 December 1905)[126]

The sixth: inner balance arising from all these other preparatory exercises. One is now ripe for inner soul schooling. One is ready to embark on the path.
(30 May 1906)[127]

[. . .] and finally, the harmony of soul life.
(6 June 1906)[128]

The sixth: inner balance and inner harmony.
(9 July 1906)[129]

Inner balance. And then, as the next quality, comes inner balance. This develops subsequently through the five other qualities, entirely by itself. We need to attend to these six qualities. We must take our life in hand and gradually progress: slowly and surely like a drop of water wearing away a stone.
(2 September 1906)[130]

Sixth: developing harmony of soul. In fact this will arise by itself through all the others.
(19 September 1906)[131]

The sixth stage consists in harmonizing the other five qualities.
(22 February 1907)[132]

⋆

During the sixth month you should try to practise all five exercises systematically in regular and repeated alternation. Gradually this will develop a fine harmony in your soul. In particular you will notice that any dissatisfaction with the world will fade. A mood grows in which the soul is reconciled with all experiences. This cannot be mistaken for indifference but, on the contrary, the capacity to work in

the world in a way which really brings about improvement or progress is dependent on it. A calm insight into things the soul previously had no access to now opens up. A person's gait and gestures will even change as the result of such exercises; and one day he may even notice that his handwriting has acquired a different character. He can then say that he has got his foot on the first step of the ladder that leads him upwards.
(General requirements, October 1906)[133]

The sixth: to repeat all five exercises in rhythmic alternation.
(20 January 1907)[134]

During the sixth period all five exercises should then be undertaken together, to create harmonious accord.
(29 January 1907)[135]

6. *Balance.* The five preceding feelings should now be brought into harmony by attending equally to all of them.
(6 June 1907)[136]

6. *Harmonizing the five stages:* The other five stages are the precondition for this sixth stage. The sequence in which they are done is extremely important. You must not try to accomplish the sixth step before the first five. Nothing can be harmonized if there is nothing there to harmonize!
(6 June 1907)[137]

6. This exercise is a combination of the preceding ones. You can undertake two at a time, or however you wish to do it.

Practising this will give you a sense of growing bigger, growing out beyond your skin.

(13 August 1908)[138]

There is no need for anyone to proceed further, since he establishes contact with the world of spirit through these five stages. But by continual repetition of these exercises one must create a combined harmony between the diverse capacities thereby achieved. This is what the sixth exercise accomplishes.

(2 January 1914)[139]

The six supplementary exercises

The exercises I have described are appropriate methods for spiritual schooling because, if carried out conscientiously, they not only bring about what has been highlighted here as their direct effect in the esoteric pupil but also, indirectly, engender many other qualities needed on the path to worlds of spirit. If you practise these exercises sufficiently they will confront you with a range of deficiencies and flaws in your psyche; but at the same time they will also furnish you with the means to consolidate and strengthen your intellect, emotional life and character. No doubt you will also need various other exercises too, depending on your capacities, temperament and character. These will develop however if you undertake the exercises referred to with sufficient perseverance. In fact, you will find that they also gradually provide things that don't initially appear inherent in them. For instance, if someone has too little self-confidence, he will discover after some time that the self-confidence he needs has in fact developed through these exercises. And the same applies to other qualities of soul. (Specific and more detailed exercises can be found in my book *Knowledge of the Higher Worlds.*) What is significant is that the spiritual pupil becomes increasingly able to enhance the described capacities to ever higher degrees.
(GA 13, 1910)[140]

For the occultist, the true initiate, it is a matter of changing the direction of his life. Nowadays people's actions are determined and driven by their sense impressions, that is, by the external world. But everything tied to space and time is without significance. We can overlook it.

What can help us achieve this goal? [The six supplementary exercises are then described.]
(6 June 1906)[141]

The supplementary exercises form the qualities we need on the physical plane, that is: control of thinking, self-determined actions, composure, etc. Gradually we will develop a corner of our heart, our soul, in which we preserve what is most sacred to us, in which we are esotericists while at the same time standing fully within external life. Battles with ourselves and with the world are inevitable here. To be an esotericist one needs to become a fighter.
(10 March 1911)[142]

We should not be dominated by greed for spiritual insight. Instead, the mood we experience when we act morally—for example when we feel compassion and selfless rejoicing—should take hold in us. Otherwise the esotericist is in grave danger of actually becoming morally weak, of becoming a worse person than he was before. For this reason the supplementary exercises for intellectual and moral consolidation and training are always also necessary alongside the meditations *per se*.
(10 March 1912)[143]

It is no less important to develop moral qualities at the same time. This is the purpose of the supplementary exercises. If you carry them out faithfully you will find that you start to develop morally. This involves combining the streams that flow in from without with what is present in your own body. *(7 June 1912)*[144]

What is the purpose of the School of Spiritual Science? It offers suggestions for ways in which we can advance quicker and more easily, for this is what humanity needs. But it is also unavoidable that this will appeal to human egotism. This is the reason for the supplementary exercises: to combat what enhances our egotism. If we neglect these, ambition and vanity will inevitably arise in the pupil. We need to observe these traits in ourselves.
(9 June 1912)[145]

These exercises are of the very greatest importance. By means of them the soul can find its way into worlds of spirit. You will find references to these five exercises everywhere in my lecture cycles and books. We wouldn't need to hold esoteric classes if everyone read them attentively and kindled the power of these exercises in their soul. They support the other, specific meditation exercises.

The esotericist has to be attentive to the smallest things. He must observe everything conscientiously as soon as he approaches worlds of spirit, though in a quite different way from observation in the physical world. In the spiritual realm things are so much more subtle and delicate than on the physical plane. For this reason the esotericist must practise these exercises continually, repeatedly finding enthusiasm for renewed efforts and new observations. Otherwise he will

be unable to gain insights into the spiritual world. Above all, the esotericist must have patience. After practising for a short while most people think they ought to be able to penetrate the spiritual world—that all gates to the world of spirit ought then to open for them.
(2 January 1914)[146]

Developing the twelve-petalled lotus flower

Spiritual science speaks of *four* qualities which must be acquired on the path of trial and initiation in order for one to ascend to higher knowledge. The first is the capacity to distinguish truth from appearance in thinking, distinguish truth from mere opinion. The second is to properly value truth and reality as opposed to appearance. The third, as mentioned already in the previous chapter, involves practising the six qualities: control of thoughts, control of actions, forbearance, steadfastness, belief and equanimity. The fourth is love of inner freedom.

We have already spoken of the six virtues composing the third quality. They are connected with development of the twelve-petalled lotus flower in the heart region.
(GA 10, 1905)[147]

I now want to speak about the twelve-petalled lotus flower in the region of the heart. Six of its petals developed already in the very ancient past, and the other six must be developed in future—in all people eventually, and today in initiates and their pupils. In all theosophical tracts you can find mention of certain virtues which must first be acquired by those who wish to rise to the level of the *chela* or spiritual pupil. These six virtues, cited in every theosophical text on self-development, are: control of thoughts, control of actions, forbearance, steadfastness, open-mindedness and balance—or what Angelus Silesius calls composure.[148] These six, virtues which one must practise consciously and attentively, and which must supplement meditation, develop the other six petals of the twelve-petalled lotus. This is not accidentally or arbitrarily included in theosophical works, is not based on someone's own inner feelings, but is drawn from the deepest knowledge of the great initiates. The initiates know that anyone who really wishes to develop to higher stages of supersensible knowledge must first develop the twelve-petalled lotus. To do so he must today develop the six petals not originally activated in the past by practising these six virtues. You can therefore see that the great initiates gave instructions and guidance for life out of deep insight into the nature of the human being. I would be able to extend these thoughts and apply them likewise to other organs of knowledge and observation, but here I only wished to give you an outline of the process of initiation.

(16 March 1905)[149]

We possess yet another lotus flower, with twelve petals, situated in the heart region. Originally only six petals were visible. Acquiring six virtues will in future develop the six other petals. These six virtues are: control of thoughts, power of initiative, soul equilibrium, positivity (which enables us to

find the best in everything), an outlook free of prejudice, and finally harmony of soul life. Then the twelve petals will start to move. They express the sacred character of the number twelve, which we rediscover in the twelve apostles, or the twelve Arthurian knights; and in each case this involves creativity and activity. This is so because everything in the world develops twelve different aspects or nuances.
(6 June 1906)[150]

Sequence and duration of the exercises

The supplementary exercises: here again we must start with thinking and continue until the relevant feeling arises; we must then pour this into the body, then practise this exercise for a month or more before proceeding to the second exercise, and so on. The astral body acquires consistency through this 'pouring', a solid form, backbone. [Then follows a description of the supplementary exercises.]

Each of these supplementary exercises should be done until one can experience the corresponding feeling and pour it into the body. Only then should one proceed to the next exercise.[151]
(20 January 1907)[152]

These exercises do not necessarily each have to be done for a month. It was just that I had to give some idea of a period. What's important above all is to do the exercises in this order. If you do the second one before the first it will have no benefit—it's the sequence that is really important. Some

people even think they should start with the sixth exercise, with harmonizing. But can you harmonize something before it even exists? If you do not do the exercises in the right sequence they will be useless. It is as if someone were crossing a bridge in six steps and tried to take the sixth step first. It would be just as senseless to try to start with the sixth exercise.
(6 June 1907)[153]

The six stages of the supplementary exercises must be done in the given sequence, for only then will they develop esoteric strength. Once you've completed the six months, start all over again. (As example, if we take six steps to cross a bridge, we can't start with the sixth step: we have to take one step after another. The sixth stage harmonizes the five preceding ones. If we tried to do this first, there would be nothing there to harmonize.)
(6 June 1907)[154]

The protective function of the supplementary exercises

Once again, two things must be accentuated:

First, that the six exercises counteract the harmful effect that other esoteric exercises can have, retaining only what is beneficial. And secondly, that they alone really safeguard the positive results of meditation and concentration work. Even ordinary, conscientious fulfilment of mundane moral standards is not sufficient for the esoteric pupil, for such morality can be very egotistic—for example if someone thinks he will

be good in order to be regarded as good. The esotericist does not do what is good in order to be seen as such, but because he gradually recognizes that goodness alone advances evolution, whereas evil, imprudence and unpleasantness put a spanner in the works of this evolution.
(General requirements, October 1906)[155]

Once someone has developed these qualities in himself, he is safe from all danger that the splitting of his nature might cause: the characteristics of his lower nature no longer affect him and he cannot deviate from the path. This is why these qualities must be developed with great precision. Then follows occult life, which gives life a certain rhythmic expression.
(7 December 1905)[156]

Control of thoughts is one of the preconditions for all higher endeavour, along with an ethical life and the effort not to give oneself up to every stirring of emotion, neither joy nor pain, but to retain equilibrium of soul. This also makes it possible for good beings to be active when the astral body is working on the physical and etheric bodies during sleep.
(26 February 1906)[157]

Today, when we work continually, pursuing every will impulse as we exercise our profession, and responding to every sensation with unregulated feeling, thinking and will, this conflict exhausts our forces. If we then wish to withdraw certain soul forces from the body, we must offer the body a substitute through certain patterns of harmonious organiza-

tion. This is why the path of self-development initially requires the inner development of certain specific virtues, so that the strength that is now withdrawn from the body is replaced by rhythm. These virtues are: control of thoughts, of actions, open-mindedness, fortitude, equanimity and trust in our whole surroundings [a description follows here of the supplementary exercises].
(19 April 1906)[158]

The virtues described are there to release higher forces for us. They make all of our lower life rhythmic, giving the soul forces that it can dedicate to higher development. This inner development occurs very quietly within.
(19 April 1906)[159]

Sleep is the starting point for developing the spiritual senses. When we are asleep, the physical and etheric bodies are lying in bed while the astral body and I are outside it. When someone starts to become clairvoyant in sleep, for a certain while forces are withdrawn which previously took care of renewing the physical and etheric body. They must be replaced by different means, if one is to avoid great danger to the physical and etheric bodies. If this does not happen, these bodies and their forces are much depleted, and amoral beings can take possession of them. It can therefore happen that despite developing astral clairvoyance, people nevertheless become immoral. [. . .]

The following is an important principle: one can leave a being or process to its own devices the more one has introduced rhythm into it. Thus the esoteric pupil must also

introduce a certain regularity into his world of thinking, inform it with rhythm. [A description of the supplementary exercises follows.]
(9 July 1906)[160]

If we develop all these qualities in ourselves, then rhythm enters our inner life in such a way that the astral body no longer needs to take care of regeneration during sleep. This is because these exercises introduce such equilibrium into the etheric body too that it can protect and renew itself. But if you embark on occult training without developing these six qualities, you will be in danger and exposed to the worst beings during the night. Once you have practised these six qualities for a while, you can start to develop your astral senses, and begin to retain consciousness when you sleep. Your dreams will no longer be arbitrary but acquire regularity, and the astral world will rise up before you.
(9 July 1906)[161]

When embarking on the path you need patience and endurance, and must be clear that you will be exposed to great dangers if you have not first undergone a rigorous character schooling. A metaphor can illustrate this: take a green fluid, a mixture of a blue and yellow fluid. You can use chemical means to separate the blue from the green again. Beforehand you saw nothing of the characteristics of the two, now separated fluids, but these are now apparent. The same is true in us. The higher and lower are combined, and the lower is protected by the higher power it is combined with from exerting its full effects. Through your exercises you can

separate the two parts. You can then find that someone who was really pretty reasonable before becomes malicious and devious, and reveals quite new, bad qualities. We must be clear about this. Such a danger can be avoided in all cases if certain preparatory exercises are undertaken, which anchor the pupil in a certain inner morality of character. [A description of the supplementary exercises follows.]
(22 February 1907)[162]

You have seen that it is indeed a reality that a kind of force arises in the physical body which gives it the capacity to become fragmented. Yet it continues to cohere, it does not succumb, for at our stage of human evolution occult practice should not go so far as to harm the physical body. Yet a degree of occult development is possible which can lead to the physical and etheric body invoking inwardly destructive powers; and basically this is always the case when we meet the Guardian of the Threshold. This encounter with the Guardian of the Threshold is not even possible without running the danger of, in a certain sense, implanting destructive forces in one's physical and etheric body. But any proper occult schooling simultaneously creates the means to counter this, and these can be found in the six supplementary exercises described in my book *Occult Science*: concentration of thoughts (i.e. strongly harnessing one's thoughts, concentrated collecting of thoughts), developing a certain will initiative, a certain equilibrium in suffering and joy, a certain positivity in relation to the world, and a certain open-mindedness. If you school these qualities in your soul alongside esoteric development, then although the physical and etheric bodies will tend towards fragmenting—in other words, absorb seeds of death under the influence of occult development—at the same time this effect will be redressed and therefore will never affect you if you develop the virtues described or if your moral development is sufficient in a way that equates with these six qualities.

(29 March 1913)[163]

The supplementary exercises and the Anthroposophical Society

If you read my book *Knowledge of the Higher Worlds,* you will find there, amongst many exercises suggested for the human soul, also six that should be done in certain repeated cycles. One of these is to cultivate a completely open mind towards the different realms of life. Yes, my dear friends, the Anthroposophical Society itself, as a whole, needs these six virtues, and we must endeavour to ensure that the Anthroposophical Society as such possesses them.

(23 January 1923)[164]

Notes and references

'GA' stands for *Gesamtausgabe* or Collected Works of Rudolf Steiner in the original German. For a list of published translations see page 87.

Prelude

1. GA 13, pp. 329 f. After this book (*Occult Science*) was published, Rudolf Steiner usually referred to it in relation to the supplementary exercises. Fundamental comments on the path of knowledge proposed by Rudolf Steiner can be found in the chapter of the same volume entitled 'Knowledge of Higher Worlds. Concerning Initiation' and also in *Knowledge of the Higher Worlds*, GA 10.

2. GA 267, p. 55. This passage comes from the text entitled 'General requirements which each person who wishes to undergo esoteric development must make of himself', which Rudolf Steiner wrote down for his esoteric pupils, for copying, in October 1906.

The first supplementary exercise

3. Translator's note: the German word is 'Gegenstand' which can mean both 'subject' and 'object'! Although Steiner often recommends concentrating on a particular *object* (pin, pencil etc.), it is by no means clear in these passages that he always means a tangible object. In several places it seems that he is referring, equally, to the possibility of focusing on a concept, theme or *subject*. In this sense, an 'object' can of course be a 'subject for reflection', which is how I frequently translate it here.

4. In Steiner's cosmology, these designations refer to previous embodiments of the earth.

5. GA 13, pp. 330 f.

6. Lotus flowers: the seven spiritual organs in the human being, also known as chakras (Sanskrit for 'wheel'). Cf. also GA 10, pp. 116 ff: 'The organ in the proximity of the larynx has sixteen "petals" or "spokes", the one close to the heart has 12, and the one in the region of the pit of the stomach has 10' (op. cit. p. 118).

7. GA 10, pp. 127 f. The text of *Knowledge of the Higher Worlds* first appeared in successive issues of the periodical edited by Rudolf Steiner and Marie von Sivers entitled *Lucifer-Gnosis*, nos. 13–28 (June 1904–September 1905). The references to the supplementary exercises are found in no. 21, February 1905. The version printed here follows the last authorized edition of GA 10.

8. GA 12, pp. 30 f. The essays collected in the book *Die Stufen der höheren Erkenntnis* first appeared in the periodical edited by Rudolf Steiner and Marie von Sivers entitled *Lucifer-Gnosis*, nos. 29, 30, 32, 34 and 35 (October 1905–May 1908). References to the supplementary exercises are found in no. 30, which bears no publication date but must have appeared at the beginning of 1906. The version printed here follows the last authorized edition of GA 12.

9. 'Chela': an Indian term common in theosophical circles at the time, meaning 'spiritual pupil'.

10. Lecture in Berlin-Schlachtensee, summer 1903, GA 88, p. 177.

11. Lecture in Berlin, 7 December 1905, GA 54, p. 213.

12. Lecture in Berlin, 19 April 1906, GA 54, p. 470.

13. Lecture in Paris, 30 May 1906, GA 94, p. 44.

14. Lecture in Leipzig, 9 July 1906, GA 94, p. 172.

15. Lecture in Stuttgart, 2 September 1906, GA 95, p. 117.

16. Lecture in Basel, 19 September 1906, GA 97, pp. 183 f.

17. Lecture in Vienna, 22 February 1907, GA 97, p. 244.

18. For the relationship between Rosicrucianism and theosophy/ anthroposophy cf. for instance GA 99, the cycle 'Theosophy and Rosicrucianism' in GA 100, and the special edition *Anthroposophie und Rosenkreuzertum* published by Rudolf Steiner Verlag.

19. Lecture in Kassel, 29 June 1907, GA 100, p. 202.

20. Lecture in Vienna, 7 November 1907, GA 98, p. 32.

21. Lecture in The Hague, 29 March 1913, GA 145, p. 193.

22. GA 267, pp. 55 f.

23. Transcript of esoteric class from memory, Stuttgart 20 January 1907, GA 266/1, p. 194.

24. Transcript of esoteric class from memory, Berlin 29 January 1907, GA 266/1, p. 202.

25. Transcript of esoteric class from memory, Munich 6 June 1907, GA 266/1, transcript A: pp. 232 f.

26. Transcript of esoteric class from memory, Munich 6 June 1907, GA 266/1, transcript B: pp. 238 f.

27. Transcript of esoteric class from memory, Stuttgart 13 August 1908, GA 266/1, p. 418.

28. Transcript of esoteric class from memory, Leipzig 2 January 1914, GA 266/3, transcript A: p. 241.

29. Transcript of esoteric class from memory, Leipzig 2 January 1914, GA 266/3, transcript C: p. 249. Cf. also transcript D of the same session: p. 258.

30. Transcript of esoteric class from memory, Hannover 7 February 1914, GA 266/3, p. 258.

In relation to the practice of control of thinking, see also comments in the esoteric classes in Berlin on 8, 15 and 21 February 1904, and 14 March 1904, in GA 266/1.

The second supplementary exercise
31. GA 13, pp. 331 f.
32. GA 10, p. 128.
33. GA 12, p. 31.
34. Lecture in Berlin-Schlachtensee, summer 1903, GA 88, pp. 177 f.
35. Lecture in Berlin, 7 December 1905, GA 54, pp. 213 f.
36. Lecture in Berlin, 19 April 1906, GA 54, p. 470.
37. Lecture in Paris, 30 May 1906, GA 94, p. 44.
38. Lecture in Leipzig, 9 July 1906, GA 94, p. 172.
39. Lecture in Stuttgart, 2 September 1906, GA 95, p. 118.
40. Lecture in Basel, 19 September 1906, GA 97, p. 184.
41. Lecture in Vienna, 22 February 1907, GA 97, p. 244.
42. Lecture in Vienna, 7 November 1907, GA 98, p. 33.
43. Lecture in The Hague, 29 March 1913, GA 145, pp. 193 f.
44. GA 267, pp. 56 f.
45. Transcript of esoteric class from memory, Stuttgart 20 January 1907, GA 266/1, p. 194.
46. Transcript of esoteric class from memory, Berlin 29 January 1907, GA 266/1, p. 202.
47. Transcript of esoteric class from memory, Munich 6 June 1907, GA 266/1, transcript A: p. 233.
48. Transcript of esoteric class from memory, Munich 6 June 1907, GA 266/1, transcript B: p. 239.
49. Transcript of esoteric class from memory, Stuttgart 13 August 1908, GA 266/1, p. 418.
50. Transcript of esoteric class from memory, Leipzig 2 January 1914, GA 266/3, transcript A: pp. 241 f.
51. Transcript of esoteric class from memory, Leipzig 2 January

1914, GA 266/3, transcript C: p. 249. Cf. also transcript D of the same session: p. 251.

52. Transcript of esoteric class from memory, Hannover 7 February 1914, GA 266/3, p. 258.

The third supplementary exercise

53. GA 13, pp. 332–4.

54. GA 10, p. 129. Here the third exercise takes the place of the sixth in the sequence.

55. GA 12, pp. 31 f.

56. Lecture in Berlin-Schlachtensee, summer 1903, GA 88, p. 178. Here the exercise usually cited as the third is placed fourth in the sequence.

57. Lecture in Berlin, 7 December 1905, GA 54, p. 214.

58. Lecture in Berlin, 19 April 1906, GA 54, p. 470.

59. Lecture in Paris, 30 May 1906, GA 94, p. 44.

60. Lecture in Leipzig, 9 July 1906, GA 94, p. 172.

61. Lecture in Stuttgart, 2 September 1906, GA 95, p. 118.

62. Lecture in Basel, 19 September 1906, GA 97, p. 184.

63. Lecture in Vienna, 22 February 1907, GA 97, p. 244.

64. Lecture in Vienna, 7 November 1907, GA 98, p. 33.

65. Lecture in The Hague, 29 March 1913, GA 145, p. 194.

66. GA 267, pp. 57 f.

67. Transcript of esoteric class from memory, Stuttgart 20 January 1907, GA 266/1, p. 194.

68. Transcript of esoteric class from memory, Berlin 29 January 1907, GA 266/1, pp. 202 f.

69. Transcript of esoteric class from memory, Munich 6 June 1907, GA 266/1, transcript A: p. 233.

70. Transcript of esoteric class from memory, Munich 6 June 1907, GA 266/1, transcript B: p. 239.

71. Transcript of esoteric class from memory, Stuttgart 13 August 1908, GA 266/1, p. 418.

72. Transcript of esoteric class from memory, Karlsruhe 14 October 1911, GA 266/2, p. 232.

73. Transcript of esoteric class from memory, Leipzig 2 January 1914, GA 266/3, transcript A: p. 243.

74. Transcript of esoteric class from memory, Leipzig 2 January 1914, GA 266/3, transcript C: pp. 249 f. Cf. also transcript D of the same session: p. 251.

75. Rudolf Steiner frequently cites the Latin verse which comes from the *Fama Fraternitatis* of 1614. In the lecture in Vienna on 11 June 1922, GA 211, p. 217, he translates it as follows: 'Ex Deo nascimur—out of God we are born. / In Christo morimur—In Christ we die. / Per Spiritum Sanctum reviviscimus—through the Holy Spirit we will re-awaken in the Spirit Self.'

76. Transcript of esoteric class from memory, Hannover 7 February 1914, GA 266/3, pp. 258 f. The transcript of this esoteric class only contains a description of the first three supplementary exercises.

The fourth supplementary exercise

77. The Persian legend repeatedly cited by Rudolf Steiner in relation to the fourth supplementary exercise can be found in Goethe's *West-East Divan*, Hamburg edition, vol. 2, p. 163, Verlag C.H. Beck, Munich 1994 (15th edition):

> Lord Jesus, who wanders through the world
> Once passed a market place and there
> A dog was lying, dead, just left
> To rot in the street before a door.
> A crowd stood round the corpse the way

That vultures flock round carrion.
One said: 'I can't think straight for the stink.'
Another: 'That's all we need: a corpse
Like this will only bring bad luck.'
Each one in his own way reviled
The dead dog's body. Then Jesus came
And spoke without revulsion, from
The goodness of his being, said:
'The teeth are white as pearls.' At which
Those standing round felt flushed with shame
Like oysters seared by warming flame.

78. GA 13, 30th edition 1989, pp. 334 f.
79. GA 10, pp. 128 f.
80. GA 12, pp. 32 f.
81. Lecture in Berlin-Schlachtensee, summer 1903, GA 88, p. 178. Here the exercise normally given as fourth in the sequence is cited as third.
82. Lecture in Berlin, 7 December 1905, GA 54, p. 214.
83. Lecture in Berlin, 19 April 1906, GA 54, pp. 470 f.
84. Lecture in Paris, 30 May 1906, GA 94, p. 44.
85. Lecture in Paris, 6 June 1906, GA 94, p. 68.
86. Lecture in Leipzig, 9 July 1906, GA 94, p. 172.
87. Lecture in Stuttgart, 2 September 1906, GA 95, pp. 118 f.
88. Lecture in Basel, 19 September 1906, GA 97, pp. 184 f.
89. Lecture in Vienna, 22 February 1907, GA 97, pp. 244 f.
90. Lecture in Kassel, 29 June 1907, GA 100, pp. 202 f. In this lecture Rudolf Steiner only highlights control of thoughts and positivity as exercises.
91. Lecture in Vienna, 7 November 1907, GA 98, pp. 33 f.
92. Lecture in The Hague, 29 March 1913, GA 145, p. 194.
93. GA 267, pp. 58 f.

94. Transcript of esoteric class from memory, Stuttgart 20 January 1907, GA 266/1, p. 194.

95. Transcript of esoteric class from memory, Berlin 29 January 1907, GA 266/1, p. 203.

96. Transcript of esoteric class from memory, Munich 6 June 1907, GA 266/1 transcript A: pp. 233 f.

97. Transcript of esoteric class from memory, Munich 6 June 1907, GA 266/1, transcript B: pp. 239 f.

98. Transcript of esoteric class from memory, Stuttgart 13 August 1908, GA 266/1, p. 418.

99. Transcript of esoteric class from memory, Leipzig, 2 January 1914, GA 266/3, transcript A: p. 243 f.

100. Transcript of esoteric class from memory, Leipzig, 2 January 1914, GA 266/3, transcript C: p. 250. Cf. also transcript D of the same session: p. 251.

Compare the fourth supplementary exercise with Rudolf Steiner's comments on: 'forbearance', 'tolerance', 'positivity' and 'understanding' in the following lectures: Berlin, 4 January 1904 in GA 52; Berlin, 23 November 1905 in GA 54; Dornach, 25 October 1918 in GA 185; Dornach, 16 February 1919 in GA 189; and Zurich, 11 February 1919 in GA 193.

The fifth supplementary exercise

101. GA 13, p. 335.

102. GA 10, p. 129.

103. GA 12, p. 33.

104. Lecture in Berlin-Schlachtensee, summer 1903, GA 88, p. 178.

105. Lecture in Berlin, 7 December 1905, GA 54, p. 215.

106. Lecture in Paris, 30 May 1906, GA 94, p. 44.

107. Lecture in Paris, 6 June 1906, GA 94, p. 68.

108. Lecture in Leipzig, 9 July 1906, GA 94, p. 172.

109. Lecture in Stuttgart, 2 September 1906, GA 95, p. 119.

110. Lecture in Basel, 19 September 1906, GA 97, p. 185.

111. Lecture in Vienna, 22 February 1907, GA 97, p. 245.

112. Lecture in Vienna, 7 November 1907, GA 98, p. 34.

113. GA 267, p. 60.

114. Transcript of esoteric class from memory, Stuttgart 20 January 1907, GA 266/1, p. 194.

115. Transcript of esoteric class from memory, Berlin 29 January 1907, GA 266/1, p. 203.

116. Transcript of esoteric class from memory, Munich 6 June 1907, GA 266/1, transcript A: p. 234.

117. Transcript of esoteric class from memory, Munich 6 June 1907, GA 266/1, transcript B: p. 240.

118. Transcript of esoteric class from memory, Stuttgart 13 August 1908, GA 266/1, pp. 418 f.

119. Transcript of esoteric class from memory, Leipzig 2 January 1914, GA 266/3, transcript A: pp. 244 f.

120. Transcript of esoteric class from memory, Leipzig 2 January 1914, GA 266/3, transcript C: p. 250. Cf. also transcript D of the same session, p. 251.

121. Transcript of esoteric class from memory, Leipzig 2 January 1914, GA 266/3, transcript D: p. 251.

The sixth supplementary exercise
122. GA 13, p. 336.

123. GA 10, p. 128. Here the sixth exercise takes the place of the third in the sequence.

124. GA 12, pp. 33 f.

125. Lecture in Berlin-Schlachtensee, summer 1903, GA 88, p. 178.

126. Lecture in Berlin, 7 December 1905, GA 54, p. 215.

127. Lecture in Paris, 30 May 1906, GA 94, p. 44.

128. Lecture in Paris, 6 June 1906, GA 94, p. 68.
129. Lecture in Leipzig, 9 July 1906, GA 94, p. 68.
130. Lecture in Stuttgart, 2 September 1906, GA 95, p. 119.
131. Lecture in Basel, 19 September 1906, GA 97, p. 185.
132. Lecture in Vienna, 22 February 1907, GA 97, p. 245.
133. GA 267, pp. 60 f.
134. Transcript of esoteric class from memory, Stuttgart 20 January 1907, GA 266/1, p. 194.
135. Transcript of esoteric class from memory, Berlin 29 January 1907, GA 266/1, p. 203.
136. Transcript of esoteric class from memory, Munich 6 June 1907, GA 266/1, transcript A: p. 234.
137. Transcript of esoteric class from memory, Munich 6 June 1907, GA 266/1, transcript B: p. 240.
138. Transcript of esoteric class from memory, Stuttgart 13 August 1908, GA 266/1, p. 419.
139. Transcript of esoteric class from memory, Leipzig, 2 January 1914, GA 266/3, transcript A: p. 245.

The six supplementary exercises
140. GA 13, pp. 336 f.
141. Lecture in Paris, 6 June 1906, GA 94, pp. 43 f.
142. Transcript of esoteric class from memory, Mannheim 10 March 1911, GA 266/2, p. 158. Cf. the similar wording of the esoteric class in Mannheim on 10 March 1912 in the same volume, p. 344.
143. Transcript of esoteric class from memory, Frankfurt 10 March 1912, GA 266/2, p. 347.
144. Transcript of esoteric class from memory, Christiania (Oslo), 7 June 1912, GA 266/2, p. 381.
145. Transcript of esoteric class from memory, Christiania (Oslo), 9 June 1912, GA 266/2, p. 386.

146. Transcript of esoteric class from memory, Leipzig 2 January 1914, GA 266/3, transcript A: p. 245.

147. GA 10, pp. 145f. Here the supplementary exercises are listed in a sequence that deviates from that in other accounts. The third takes the place of what is usually the sixth, and *vice versa*. The corresponding passage first appeared in *Lucifer-Gnosis*, no. 22, March 1905.

148. Johannes Scheffler, known as Angelus Silesius ('Silesian messenger') was a religious thinker and poet. In his *Cherubinian Wanderer* the complex concept of composure is first elaborated.

149. Lecture in Berlin, 16 March 1905, GA 53, pp. 265 f.

150. Lecture in Paris, 6 June 1906, GA 94, pp. 68 f.

151. Translator's note: Steiner uses the word 'month' here, rather than 'exercise'.

152. Transcript of esoteric class from memory, Stuttgart 20 January 1907, GA 266/1, p. 194.

153. Transcript of esoteric class from memory, Munich 6 June 1907, GA 266/1, transcript A: p. 234.

154. Transcript of esoteric class from memory, Munich 6 June 1907, GA 266/1, transcript B: p. 238.

155. GA 267, p. 61.

156. Lecture in Berlin, 7 December 1905, GA 54, pp. 215 f.

157. Lecture in Berlin, 26 February 1906, GA 94, p. 203.

158. Lecture in Berlin, 19 April 1906, GA 54, pp. 469 f.

159. Op. cit. p. 471.

160. Lecture in Leipzig, 9 July 1906, GA 94, pp. 171 f.

161. Op. cit. p. 172.

162. Lecture in Vienna, 22 February 1907, GA 97, pp. 243 f.

163. Lecture in The Hague, 29 March 1913, GA 145, pp. 193 f.

164. Lecture in Stuttgart, 23 January 1923, GA 257, p. 25.

Sources

The following volumes are cited in this book. Where relevant, published editions of equivalent English translations are given below the German titles.

The works of Rudolf Steiner are listed with the volume numbers of the complete works in German, the *Gesamtausgabe* (GA), as published by Rudolf Steiner Verlag, Dornach, Switzerland.

RSP = Rudolf Steiner Press, UK
AP / SB = Anthroposophic Press / SteinerBooks, USA

10   *Wie erlangt man Erkenntnisse der höheren Welten?*
      Knowledge of the Higher Words (RSP); *How to Know Higher Worlds* (SB)

12   *Die Stufen der höheren Erkenntnis*
      Stages of Higher Knowledge (AP)

13   *Die Geheimwissenschaft im Umriss*
      Occult Science (RSP); *An Outline of Esoteric Science* (SB)

52   *Spirituelle Seelenlehre und Weltbetrachtung*
      Spiritualism, Madame Blavatsky and Theosophy (SB)

53   *Sprung und Ziel des Menschen*

54   *Die Welträtsel und die Anthroposophie*

88   *Über die astral Welt und das Devachan*

94   *Kosmogonie*
      An Esoteric Cosmology (Garber Communications)

95   *Vor dem Tore der Theosophie*
      Founding a Science of the Spirit (RSP)

97   *Das christliche Mysterium*
      The Christian Mystery (Completion Press)

98   *Natur- und Geistwesen—Ihr Wirken in unserer sichtbaren Welt*

All English-language titles are available via Rudolf Steiner Press, UK (www.rudolfsteinerpress.com) or SteinerBooks, USA (www.steinerbooks.org)

ALSO AVAILABLE:

Rudolf Steiner
Strengthening the Will
The 'Review Exercises'

The so-called 'review exercises'—to be carried out alongside the 'supplementary exercises' and meditation—are integral to the path of personal development and knowledge presented by Rudolf Steiner. Together they form a means of experiencing the spiritual realm in full consciousness. Meditation enlivens *thinking*, the supplementary exercises educate and balance *feeling*, whilst the review exercises cultivate the *will* by penetrating it with powers of consciousness. Conscientiously practised, this path of self-knowledge and development has the effect of opening a source of inner strength and psychological health that soon make themselves felt in daily life.

The review exercises bring the experiences of our daily lives to full awareness. By directing our attentive gaze to what has happened—whether in a single day or in whole phases of life—we kindle light in our will. Undertaking such a review *backwards*, in reverse sequence, or from an 'external perspective', requires a huge inner effort as we establish distance between ourselves and our daily experiences.

In this essential handbook the editor has drawn together virtually all Rudolf Steiner's statements on the review exercises, supporting them with commentary and notes. Described from different perspectives and approaches, there are a surprising range of suggestions for carrying them out. Individual chapters focus on reviewing the day (transforming the power of memory); reviewing events in your life (awakening the higher self); reviewing the other's perspective (awakening social impulses); exercises in thinking backwards (illuminating the will); review exercises to comprehend karmic connections; review exercises and kamaloka; and the relationship of review exercises and education.

112 pages; 978 1 85584 238 0; £9.99